Inside the Real Estate Deal

Also by Peter G. Miller

Buy Your First Home Now

The Common-Sense Mortgage

Successful Real Estate Negotiation
(with Douglas M. Bregman)

Successful Real Estate Investing

Inside the Real Estate Deal

How to Make Big Money from the Real Estate Revolution of the 1990s

Peter G. Miller

HarperCollins*Publishers*

Library of Congress Cataloging-in-Publication Data
Miller, Peter G.
    Inside the real estate deal : how to make big money from the real estate revolution of the 1990s / Peter G. Miller.
        p.   cm.
    Includes index.
    ISBN 0-06-016525-1
    1. Real estate investment.   I. Title.
HD1382.5.M55   1991
332.63′24—dc20   90-55935

91 92 93 94 95 CC/RRD 10 9 8 7 6 5 4 3 2 1

To Caroline

Contents

Acknowledgments

This book would not have been possible without the assistance of many individuals and organizations who graciously provided materials and information, arranged interviews with leading real estate authorities, and patiently answered numerous questions.

In particular, the author wishes to thank Jeffrey Lubar, Vice President, Public Affairs, and Elizabeth Duncan, Director, Media Affairs, the National Association of Realtors; Joe Nigg, Executive Editor, RE/MAX International; Monte Helm, Vice President, Publications and Public Relations, Century 21 Real Estate Corporation; and DeAnne Flynn, Corporate Public Relations Director, Help-U-Sell, Inc.

Source material for this book includes the following:

Chapter 1: Selected material concerning listings, homogeneity, the uniqueness of property and deals, and other matters originally appeared in material privately published by the author and in weekly columns written for *The Washington Post.*

Chapter 1: The hourglass system of competition was originally mentioned within a speech given by the author at a 1978 seminar entitled "Housing in North America and the Public Interest" sponsored by the Institute for Canadian-American Studies (Windsor, Ontario, Canada) and subsequently published in the Institute's proceedings.

Chapter 1: The quotation from the draft material on RESPA is taken from "RESPA—Section 14a, The Real Estate Settlement Procedures Act," Volume II, page IX.27, a study funded by HUD.

Chapter 1: The 1983 Federal Trade Commission information cited in this chapter is from page 22 of a staff report by the FTC's Los Angeles regional office entitled, "The Residential Real Estate Brokerage Industry."

Chapter 4: The 6-percent pre-tax profit margin from mid-sized realty firms can be found on page 69 in the book, *Real Estate Brokerage, 1988,* published by the National Association of Realtors.

Chapter 8: The study showing the number of brokers used by homebuyers was originally published in *REALTOR NEWS* (March 4, 1985) under the title, "Most homebuyers, sellers use service of real estate practitioner."

Chapter 9: The concept of a listing clause to anticipate possible buyer broker conflicts was privately published in 1984 within a guide written by Douglas M. Bregman, Esq. and the author entitled, *"Buyer's Brokerage: A Practical Guide for Real Estate Buyers, Brokers and Investors."* ($6.95, Tremont Press, Suite 800 West, 7315 Wisconsin Avenue, Bethesda, MD 20814)

Chapter 9: The reference to the NAR *Handbook on Multiple Listing Policy* is taken from material dated November, 1989.

Chapter 9: Portions of the material on buyer brokerage were originally written by the author and published in *Real Estate Business* (Fall, 1986), a quarterly magazine produced by the Real Estate Brokerage Council and the Residential Sales Council of the Realtors National Marketing Institute. The article was originally entitled, "Buyer Brokerage: The Other Side of the Coin."

Chapter 10: The 1987 NAR self-sellers survey was originally published in *The Homebuying and Selling Process, 1987,* part of the Real Estate Business Series published by the National Association of Realtors.

Chapter 11: The concept for a community listing service was originally outlined by the author within consulting materials developed in 1989.

Chapter 12: Portions of the material concerning fees to

brokers for mortgage information and advice originally appeared in the author's regular column in *The Real Estate Professional* (July/August, 1990) (Wellesley Publications, Inc., P.O. Box 6, Winchester, MA 01890).

Chapter 13: The material on term licensing was written by the author and originally appeared in *Real Estate Washington* (May/June 1979).

Part IV: The article entitled "Real Estate Brokers: Avoiding the Big Guy" was written by the author and originally appeared in *The Washington Post* (April 4, 1981).

Within this book are proprietary marks owned by individual organizations, including:

The term "Realtor" is a registered collective membership mark which may be used only by members of the National Association of Realtors. (430 North Michigan Avenue, Chicago, IL 60611).

The term "Help-U-Sell" is a registered service mark of Help-U-Sell, Inc. (57 West 200 South, Salt Lake City, Utah 84145).

The term "RE/MAX" is a registered trademark of RE/MAX International, Inc. (P.O. Box 3907, Englewood, CO 80155-3907).

The term "CENTURY 21" is a registered mark belonging to the Century 21 Real Estate Corporation. Readers should be aware that although generally described as "Century 21," there are, in reality, two entities involved: the Century 21 Real Estate Corporation, which is the master franchisor; and, the Century 21 system of 7,000 independently-owned and operated franchisee offices in the United States and abroad. (P.O. Box 19564, Irvine, CA 92713-9564)

Books are collaborative projects and I am fortunate to be associated with HarperCollins and its many talented people. In particular, I am grateful for the consistent support and encouragement of the editors with whom I have worked during this project; Terry Karten, Susan Randol, and Deborah Brody.

Preface

This book was written in the spirit of exploration, to record the changes that now mark the real estate industry, to show how various groups are affected, and to suggest where profit and opportunity may be found.

The first part of the book explores how the real estate business works in theory and in fact. The second part examines specific areas within brokerage where change has occurred, is occurring, and may occur in the future.

The third part contains a series of question and answer interviews with some of the leading thinkers, innovators, and executives in the real estate business. Without their participation this book would be greatly diminished and I am grateful for their willingness to share ideas with readers nationwide.

In part four, there is an article from 1981 predicting how the real estate industry might look ten years later.

This book is the fifth in a series that examines the real estate business. Other books published by HarperCollins that complement this volume include *The Common-Sense Mortgage, Successful Real Estate Investing, Successful Real Estate Negotiation,* and *Buy Your First Home Now.*

I am grateful to the many people who have written and spoken to me over the years, and for the acceptance which the books in this series have gained. To those who read these words, whether buyer or seller, or broker or agent, I wish you every success in the new age of real estate.

PETER G. MILLER
Silver Spring, MD

Inside the Real Estate Deal

PART I
Where We Stand Today

"Why do brokers get so much money?" is usually both a question and an accusation, an effort to grasp why homesellers throughout the country routinely pay thousands of dollars for real estate services, sometimes more than the cost of a new car.

Not only are buyers and sellers curious, but so too are brokers and agents. Commissions, which seem so large to consumers, rarely produce great wealth for those within the brokerage community.

If brokerage fees were a minor home-selling expense then minimal compensation levels would be understandable. But when the sale of a $150,000 home generates a commission worth $9,000, and when houses selling for $150,000 are actually cheap in many areas, then the combination of steep selling costs and small brokerage incomes seems strange. Something doesn't make sense, and that "something" is the way homes have traditionally been marketed.

Today the real estate business is evolving and old traditions are dead or dying. Those who know how to work the current system are finding bigger profits when they sell, smaller costs when they buy, and larger profits from brokerage itself.

To see why the real estate business is in flux—and to see who has benefited and who has fallen behind—we need first to look at the old days, a time not so long ago when brokerage was a very different business.

1

The Hidden Revolution

Each year the American public spends more than $20 billion to purchase services from an industry that is little understood, often maligned, and lightly regarded by many. We buy, rent and sell from real estate brokers and their agents, we decide with their help where we'll live and, really, how we'll live, and we do this in an environment in which consumer awareness has traditionally been absent.

In the past it made little difference who sold our homes or how the system worked. We could safely ask a friend, neighbor or co-worker to market a home, never fearing that a better deal was available elsewhere because virtually all brokers charged identical fees, used the same contracts, and provided services that were indistinguishable.

Today the world has changed. In the past decade new forms of competition, compensation and service have evolved, old firms have been replaced by new players, and consumers have more choices than ever before.

Yet despite massive change, many people continue to view the brokerage system through the prism of old perceptions and outdated experiences. They buy, sell and offer services at a disadvantage, not recognizing that the brokerage business of the 1990s is new and different, sometimes radically so. Steeper housing costs and smaller incomes are the penalties paid by those who do not understand how the industry has evolved.

The standards and practices which dominated real estate for so many years are changed, changing, or gone. A business that once rewarded inefficiency, lauded conformity, and inhibited meaningful competition is being transformed into a tough and competitive industry.

What caused the industry to change? Why are the old stereotypes dead or dying? To answer these questions it's best to start with real estate competition prior to 1980.

THE OLD DAYS

For much of the past 75 years real estate brokerage has been dominated by what is best described as the hourglass system of competition. At one end were great numbers of brokers and agents seeking listings and sales. On the other side were millions of owners trying to market their homes at the lowest possible cost. Rather than fully compete for these sellers, most brokers offered services only within a tight "zone of competition" defined by past practices and peer pressures—the bottleneck of the hourglass.

Brokers operating within the traditional zone of competition offered uniform commission schedules, identical listing terms, and a common set of services. While there was competition to sell these nearly identical service packages, such "competition" did not result in lower costs, better service, or greater choices to the public.

Within the industry those who attempted to offer lower prices or a different package of services were often intimidated and harassed. The official posture of the industry was absolutely clear: price and product uniformity were central to the conduct of the profession, a view reflected among "regulatory agencies" that were supposed to oversee the industry and "protect the public." As the official manual of the District of Columbia Real Estate Commission said, a broker "should respect the schedule of fees established by custom in his community."

The vehicle that allowed brokers to exert peer pressure was often the local multiple listing system (MLS). The system worked this way:

- Broker Anderson lists a home to sell for $100,000. If he sells the house, Anderson receives a 6-percent fee.

The Public View

In 1990 when the Gallup Poll surveyed a cross section of
Americans to rate 25 professions in terms of honesty and
ethical standards, druggists and pharmacists came in first,
car salesmen finished last and real estate agents placed
20th.

Percent Saying Very High or High—Trend

	1976	1977	1981	1983	1985	1988	1990
Druggists/pharmacists	NA	NA	59	61	65	66	62
Clergy	NA	61	63	64	67	60	55
Medical doctors	56	51	50	52	58	53	52
Dentists	NA	NA	52	51	56	51	52
College teachers	49	46	45	47	53	54	51
Engineers	49	46	48	45	53	48	50
Policemen	NA	37	44	41	47	47	49
Funeral directors	NA	26	30	29	32	24	35
Bankers	NA	39	39	38	38	26	32
TV reporters/ commentators	NA	NA	36	33	33	22	32
Journalists	33	33	32	28	31	23	30
Business executives	20	19	19	18	23	16	25
Newspaper reporters	NA	NA	30	26	29	22	24
Senators	19	19	20	16	23	19	24
Lawyers	25	26	25	24	27	18	22
Local office holders	NA	14	14	16	18	14	21
Building contractors	23	18	19	18	21	22	20
Congressmen	14	16	15	14	20	16	20
State office holders	NA	11	12	13	15	11	17
Real estate agents	NA	13	14	13	15	13	16
Labor union leaders	12	13	14	12	13	14	15
Stockbrokers	NA	NA	21	19	20	13	14
Insurance salesmen	NA	15	11	13	10	10	13
Advertising practitioners	11	10	9	9	12	7	12
Car salesmen	NA	8	6	6	5	6	6

SOURCE: *The Gallup Poll*

- But, Anderson may not have a buyer. In order to sell the property as quickly as possible, he tells other brokers that the house is available by listing it in a local MLS. And to induce their cooperation he offers to pay a fee, typically 50 percent of his commission (3 percent of the sale price in this example).

Rather than simply include the commission that another broker would receive for finding a purchaser (say 3 percent), many MLS networks required brokers to publish the entire commission (6 percent in our example).

Publication alerted all members in the system to the fees charged by other brokers and discouraged alternative fee arrangements. A draft study completed for the Department of Housing and Urban Affairs (HUD) came to this conclusion.

> Brokerage firms do not appear to act independently in establishing their pricing strategies. Rather, the historic evolution of industry pricing seems to influence current decisions, and to help maintain the current commission rate structure. Moreover, the mechanism of the MLS and cooperative practices seem to encourage uniform pricing and serve as a monitoring device for member firms. In many instances, they may discourage firms from reducing commission rates from those prevailing in the area.

However it was done, real estate fees were remarkably uniform.

- In a 1977 survey of the Northern Virginia suburbs outside Washington, DC, Michael Carney reported that of 1,000 homes represented for sale by local brokers, 97.6 percent were listed with a fee of at least 6 percent.
- Nationwide, a report by the Los Angeles office of the Federal Trade Commission found that "most brokers charged the customary fee in their local areas—usually 6 or 7 percent."

While peer pressure did much to assure price and service uniformity within the industry, outside the industry there was an important contributing factor: public ignorance.

For most people a real estate transaction is a rare event, something that may happen once in a decade. Because buying and selling real estate are infrequent occurrences, there is little opportunity to gain experience and such experience as one may have is unlikely to have significant value many years later.

One way to supplement experience is to obtain information from the media. In the past, however, the real estate industry also had an effective monopoly in this area in part because many newspaper real estate sections were controlled or produced by advertising departments.

A 1978 study of 42 newspaper real estate sections nationwide by the Housing Research Group of the Center for Study of Responsive Law found that, "most real estate sections serve the real estate industry far better than they serve consumers and general readers. Real estate sections too often simply repeat industry sales pitches, and too seldom provide useful information to the general reader and housing consumer. Apparently their purpose is not to inform, but to sell."

In looking at the real estate industry, its regulators and the media in the 1970s, it is important not to view events in isolation. The competitive situation in real estate wasn't great, but then it wasn't unique or even the worst that could be found.

- Virtually all professions fixed prices at the time.
- The media generally did not look at price competition in any industry or profession.
- Many professions went beyond price-fixing to set rates. One ruse, for example, was to ban advertising by professionals, a policy that cut operating costs and made it difficult for newcomers to get business.

ODDITIES

Price equality—having everyone, or almost everyone pay the same fee—had the effect of transferring benefits to the least deserving players in the marketplace.

- The broker who did a top-rate job could charge no more than the broker who provided poor service.
- The seller with the well-maintained house that was easy to sell paid the same fee as the homeowner who never

painted or made repairs and had a home that was difficult to market.

- The seller whose house sold in two days paid the same fee as the property owner whose house took six months to unload.
- The owner of a $100,000 house that was sold directly by a broker was charged the same fee as the owner of a $100,000 house that required two brokers to sell.

Uniform pricing created a calm environment where services could be sold with a minimum of conflict and competition. However, the system also made it impossible to maximize profits.

A certain number of brokers and agents always have substantial incomes, if only because in a population of more than 2 million licensees the odds are that somebody, somewhere, will do well. Generally, however, figures from one highly-reliable source with an interest in such matters suggests that brokers and agents often fared poorly.

Preliminary IRS statistics for 1988 show that 688,750 individuals reported earnings as brokers and agents. Their gross revenues were $18.992 billion, but net income—money retained after expenses—was $8.313 billion, or an average annual income of just over $12,000. Of the more than 2 million people with real estate licenses, the vast majority either had no income from brokerage activities or failed to report it.

The problem was that while fees were rarely reduced under the old system, they were impossible to raise. With a limit on fee income, brokers could only prosper by completing more transactions or by selling more expensive properties. Unfortunately, while there were only so many deals to go around, the number of brokers and agents kept growing because the standards to obtain a license were minimal. In many jurisdictions, experience was not required, there were no educational standards, and a broker's license could be obtained by taking a short exam. I know. I obtained a broker's license in 1978.

COURTLY EVENTS

The competitive issues which defined real estate had not gone unnoticed. Prior to 1980 more than 40 civil cases that involved real estate price fixing had been settled with consent decrees, evidence at least that the issue was widespread.

Congress changed the rules in 1974. That year Congress said that violations of the Sherman Antitrust Act of 1890 could be regarded as felonies rather than misdemeanors. This change was important because far stiffer penalties were possible, and the evidence used in a criminal trial could also be used in a civil suit, nasty proceedings where treble damages were possible. In contrast, the old consent decrees were civil actions. When a consent decree was accepted it was commonly agreed that evidence from the case would not be released and therefore anyone else who wanted to sue a brokerage group would have to gather their own evidence.

In 1975 James Jefferson McLain (and others) claimed that real estate fees in New Orleans were fixed and sued two real estate trade associations, six real estate companies and a number of individual brokers as a group.

The brokers' defense, in essence, was that they could not be sued under the Federal Sherman Antitrust Act because the purchase and sale of real estate was a local matter conducted entirely within the state of Louisiana.

The case reached the Supreme Court, and in a 1980 decision (known generally as McLain vs. the Real Estate Board of New Orleans) the Court decided that while it may be true that buying and selling property is a local matter, it is within the stream of interstate commerce.

Why? Because real estate deals commonly involve out-of-state services such as VA and FHA loans, mortgages from lenders across the country, and title insurance from distant companies. Given the logic of the McLain decision, it is difficult to imagine any profession or industry that is not involved in interstate commerce and therefore not subject to the Sherman Antitrust Act.

Recognizing the principles established in the McLain case, other professions saw that they too could be liable for once-standardized practices that effectively restrained trade and limited price competition. It is because of the McLain decision that we now have forms of competition not seen 20 years ago such as legal clinics, ads for physicians, and 1-hour eyewear outlets owned by corporations.

DINNER FOR SIX

Among the many people affected by the McLain decision were six real estate brokers from Montgomery County, Maryland, just a few miles from the headquarters of the Justice Department and its Antitrust Division in Washington, D.C.

The brokers were indicted by the federal government in 1977 for price fixing. It was alleged that during a 1974 dinner at a local country club, one broker said he was raising his fee from 6 percent to 7 percent. Then, the government maintained, real estate fees within the county began to rise, in part because of events set in motion by the dinner.

The government won and the brokers and their firms were fined a total of $200,000. The principle established in the McLain case—the idea that real estate transactions were within the stream of interstate commerce—had now been transformed into a hard reality.

Once the government won the Montgomery criminal case, the accused brokers had another problem. Evidence from the criminal trial could be used in a civil suit and if the brokers lost triple damages were possible. Rather than another round of costly litigation, a class-action settlement was devised to resolve all claims as follows:

- Certificates were created for each homeowner who sold a house through one of the six brokers during a three-year period.
- The certificates, or script, could be used to buy real estate services with a 1-percent discount. In other words, a seller who negotiated a 6-percent fee could turn in a certificate and the broker's fee would be reduced to 5 percent.
- The certificates could be sold. Someone with a $100,000 home would only get $1,000 by using the certificate, but if the script was sold to the owner of a $500,000 property, then it was worth far more than $1,000.

Three years after the script program was established the results were that of the 3,300 potential beneficiaries who might have qualified for discount coupons, only 1,800 could be found. Of the 1,800 certificates issued, a total of eight were redeemed.

CHANGES

The McLain decision and the Montgomery County case ended the old days of real estate. Price-fixing was no longer something that could be resolved with winks and consent decrees.

But if the old system was no longer acceptable, then what would replace it?

One practice that quickly vanished was the publication of full commissions. Under the new system homes are simply listed with a co-op fee showing how much a broker could receive for bringing in a buyer. The full fee is unknown; brokers can bargain in private and make whatever deals they like.

With the new system a broker can structure a deal with several commissions. Certainly it is still possible to share commissions on a 50/50 basis, but it is also possible to be more creative and competitive.

For example, to get a listing broker Charles might agree to a 6-percent fee if he sells a home with help from another broker. He might also agree to a 5-percent fee if he lists and sells the property by himself.

In addition to commissions, many traditional practices and understandings have also changed.

Under the old system brokers and agents typically split fees on a 50/50 basis. If agent Reynolds went from broker Green to broker Lake, the split was still likely to be 50/50, so Reynolds had little incentive to change brokers. Now brokers either pay better splits for top agents or lose out to more aggressive brokers.

If co-op fees and commission splits are no longer uniform, then what about commission rates for homeowners? Where are the stone tablets that say every broker should charge the same fee? Who says all brokers should provide the same package of services to every client? The answer to these questions can be seen in the growing number of alternative brokers, some who offer individual services on a flat-fee basis and others who simply sell services at a discount.

And, if we're going to change the way we sell services, why not go all the way and sell services to buyers? They have checkbooks, they comprise 50 percent of all real estate consumers, and they have rarely been represented by brokers in the past.

If brokers can represent either sellers or buyers, then who do they represent in individual transactions? In the past brokers worked for sellers almost exclusively, a fact largely unknown to buyers.

A 1983 staff report from the Federal Trade Commission showed that 74 percent of all purchasers believed that brokers worked for them, not sellers, a serious misunderstanding when one considers that brokers are obligated to get the best possible price and terms for their clients and that their clients are typically sellers.

Today the issue of representation is fairly clear. More than 30 states require brokers to provide disclosure forms. Such forms tell buyers that brokers work for sellers (if that is the case) and that brokers are obligated to get the best possible deals for client sellers.

However, for an increasing number of buyers and sellers such information is not news. Journalists, rather than ad departments, now control the real estate sections in most newspapers, which means that real estate matters are now covered with depth, clarity, and an adversarial attitude. Information is now available regarding fees, listing agreements, alternative brokers and self-selling, coverage that sometimes leads cave-dwelling brokers from the dark ages to complain about "negative" news.

CHANGE EQUALS OPPORTUNITY

The changes that revolutionized the real estate industry in the 1980s did not happen immediately or at once, and the result has been a gap between perception and reality. In many cases the perception is that the real estate business operates as it did 10 and 20 years ago. It doesn't. The reality is that today's brokerage business has evolved, but perhaps not in ways which either reformers or traditionalists might have expected.

- Sellers will find that variable commission rates do not necessarily mean lower fees. Those who own more desirable properties can get better deals. Those with less attractive properties should pay more, and they will.
- Buyers will discover that a growing number of brokers want to represent their interests and not those of sellers.

Buyers may also discover that brokerage fees, like other professional costs, are not cheap.

- Consumers generally will know more about real estate matters because more information is now available.
- Individuals with an interest in real estate will find that entrance requirements remain minimal. Classes and exams are now required, and standards will undoubtedly be toughened, but when compared with other fields the bottom-line requirements for an agent's license remain soft. This is good news for those who would like to consider real estate as a career option.
- Although there are few barriers to entering the industry, continuing education classes, professional seminars, and a much stronger emphasis on training means that today's brokers and agents are likely to be better educated and more skilled than practitioners of yesteryear. If they aren't better trained, then they are more likely to be sued.
- Agents will find that if they are productive they can command better commission splits than in the past. Conversely, if pay-for-performance is the principle that guides real estate fees, then new agents and seasoned professionals who do not produce will receive smaller splits than they might have earned in the past.
- Brokers will encounter a new world that includes everything from price and product competition to internal battles over agents and their compensation. Many MLS networks will admit all brokers, not just those affiliated with particular professional groups, and new MLS listing arrangements will become increasingly acceptable.
- Antitrust lawyers will have to find a new line of work. Real estate in the 1990s will be open and competitive, a capitalist's reverie.

2

Real Estate in Theory

One of the best ways to make money in America is to help others buy and sell property. Sell eight homes with an average price of $125,000, charge a 6-percent fee, and collect $60,000. Not bad, especially when the average family makes just over $32,000 a year.

The catch is that real estate economics are only simple for some people. To collect that $60,000 you must list and sell properties without help from other brokers and agents. You must be a broker, not an agent, otherwise your income will be split with someone else. And even if you are a broker, whatever you earn will be reduced by such costs as advertising, office rent, and MLS fees.

There is money to be made in real estate, but the whole story cannot be explained with simple economics. To profit and prosper there must be an understanding of how the system works, something Adams learned when he decided to become a real estate agent.

MORE THAN MONEY

When it came time for Adams to settle on his new home there was one figure that stuck out. The owner had paid $9,000 to sell his home.

The home Adams bought was not a palace or an estate. It was

worth $150,000, about average for his community. Also aver-
age, as Adams discovered, was the brokerage fee. Almost everyone used a broker and every broker in town seemed to charge
the same 6-percent fee.

As he spoke to brokers and attended career night programs
Adams kept hearing the same message: Get a license. It's easy.
Just take a 60-hour course, pass the state exam, and work with
a broker.

Nobody said openly that big paychecks were guaranteed or
promised that incomes would double, but an unmistakable message was there. Teachers, psychologists, Army officers, and
nurses all told how they made more money in real estate than
in professions requiring years of training and experience.

Sure they had to work hard, but what business is easy? At
least in real estate there are no salary caps, no 9-to-5 routines,
and no commuting. You could be your own boss and go as far
as your talent and enterprise might allow.

It sounded good and Adams wanted the money and freedom
that real estate represented. Excited and eager, he started his
first class just a few weeks later.

FIGURING THE ODDS

"You're here," said the instructor, a local broker named Hoffman, "because you see houses for sale in every neighborhood.
You read the paper and see that some agent sold property
worth $10 million last year and that looks pretty good.

"You're not here to cure cancer or save the world. You're
here to earn a few dollars, feed your family, and maybe develop
a new career. These are all fair goals, but most of you won't
make it.

"There are 60 of you in this room," Hoffman continued, "and
if you get the results I usually see, then 50 will complete this
course, 40 will take the state exam, 32 will pass on the first
attempt, and 25 will sign up with local brokers.

"Of the 25 who enter the business, most will make less than
$10,000 a year, but it's also possible that one of you will earn
more than $50,000 within the next 12 months.

"It's also true," said Hoffman, "that five years from now
maybe two or three of you will still be in the business. But if you

---

Who Are these People?

In real estate it is entirely possible to find a single individual who is an agent, broker and Realtor—all at the same time. Here is a quick guide to real estate players.

Agent. 1. A salesperson who works under the authority of a broker. 2. A broker who works for a client or principal.

Broker. An individual licensed to represent someone else for a fee in the purchase, sale, exchange, management, and leasing of real estate.

Buyer Agent. A broker who represents a purchaser.

Client (or Principal). Someone, such as a property owner, who hires a broker.

Customer. Someone, such as a buyer, who is not a client.

Listing Broker. A broker who obtains a listing contract from a homeowner.

Realtor. A registered collective membership mark that may be used only by members of the National Association of Realtors (NAR).

Selling Broker. A broker who finds a buyer.

Subagent. A broker who gains the right to show a property by operating under the authority of another broker's listing agreement.

---

are, and if you're good, you might earn more than your doctor or lawyer."

Adams thought about Hoffman and realized something was unsaid. True, an agent's license could lead to a career, but even if it didn't, the information learned from Hoffman's course—or just about any licensure course—would at least explain how real estate is bought and sold. And once he understood how the system worked, Adams was certain that he would never pay $9,000 to sell a home.

PRINCIPLES

"When you play baseball," said Hoffman, "you play with certain rules. Three strikes and you're out. Whoever is ahead after nine innings wins. Catch a fair ball and the batter is out.

"In real estate," Hoffman continued, "there are also rules that create an orderly business system. But while the rules may vary somewhat from state to state, the principles which govern brokerage activities are common throughout the country."

As he continued to speak, Hoffman gave each student a hand-out. He had made a list of 10 basic principles that explained how the real estate business worked, information that Hoffman said was used daily by brokers and agents.

1. *Brokers outrank agents.* There are two types of real estate licenses: those for brokers and those for agents. A *broker* can act independently, assist buyers and sellers directly, and collect a fee for his or her work. *Agents,* in contrast, can only operate under a broker's supervision.

Importance. Brokers call the shots in real estate. Agents listen. Seen another way, brokers are responsible for the agents they supervise.

2. *Brokers are agents.* In the usual situation, brokers do not sell or buy real estate for their own account, they assist others. When a broker assists a property owner, the seller is a *principal* or *client* and the buyer is a *customer.* If a broker represents a purchaser, then the buyer is the client.

Importance. When a broker acts as an agent, he or she has a "fiduciary" obligation to a client, a big word which basically means that a broker must act as a trustee and place the client's interests first.

What is expected from a broker? As a trustee of the client's best interests, brokers and their agents have four central obligations.

- To use care when handling the client's affairs.
- To follow lawful directions.
- To account for money and papers. For example, as the seller's agent, a broker will typically hold deposit money in an "escrow" or trust account. This money is separate from the broker's funds and cannot be released without permission from both the buyer and seller.
- To act loyally.

Being an agent is complicated by an unpleasant fact. It is possible to become an agent with a written agreement, and is also possible to become an agent with words and deeds.

Imagine if broker Thompson lists the Reynolds house, but tells buyer Tate, "Look, don't worry about a thing. Reynolds wants $150,000 but I think you should offer $140,000. Trust me, I can help you get a better deal."

In this situation Thompson is an agent for both Reynolds and Tate. He is also in deep trouble.

As an agent, Thompson has an obligation to get the best possible deal for his client, but in this scenario who is his client? He represents the seller but he is helping the buyer by suggesting a lower purchase price. Without prior disclosure or written approval from both the buyer and the seller, Thompson is an *undisclosed dual agent* who can face lawsuits by Tate, Reynolds, or both.

Is it possible to be a dual agent and not have problems? In a small number of situations brokers can act as *disclosed dual agents.* For example, if a broker arranges an exchange of properties and has written permission in advance to work for both parties, then a dual agency can be acceptable.

3. *There are often agents and subagents in real estate.* Many real estate transactions involve not one broker, but two.

To understand how this works imagine a movie where most actors have one role, but some play two parts.

- If broker Mason lists the Webster home, Mason is Webster's *agent.* Mason is also the *listing broker.*
- If broker McDonald knows a buyer and wants to show the Webster home, he can work with Mason. MacDonald is the *selling broker.* He is also a *subagent.*

What is a subagent? Mason has a contract to sell the Webster property so there is a direct connection between Mason and Webster. MacDonald may never have met Webster, but his authority to sell the property comes from whatever listing Mason has with the owner.

Importance. Because of subagency, a newly-formed real estate company can join a local multiple listing service (MLS) and immediately have the right to sell properties listed by competing brokers. In comparison, you don't see Sears and K-Mart trying to sell each other's inventory.

4. *All deals are unique.* In a free and open market a prop-

erty's selling price is determined at one point in time under specific conditions through the agreement of an informed buyer and a knowledgeable seller. At any other point in time, with other conditions, or with different buyers and sellers, the selling price can be different.

Importance. All deals are unique and all properties are different, so there is no way to prove that broker Jones can sell a property faster or for a better price than broker Smith. There is also no way to establish that one particular selling concept is better than another.

5. *All deals must be on paper.* It is entirely possible to have an oral real estate contract, a deal from the Old West where Slim says to Luke, "I'll sell the back forty for $200."

But what if Slim and Luke later forget their exact agreement? Was it the back forty east of the river, or west? Was that $200 in cash, or will Slim need a loan? Rather than argue and debate, real estate deals are made in writing in order to be enforceable.

Importance. Oral promises should be regarded as worthless.

Also, because real estate agreements are contracts, precise writing is required, a job often reserved for attorneys.

6. *Because of their police powers, states have the right to regulate real estate brokerage.* Brokers and agents in all states are licensed because such regulation is believed to protect the public interest.

Importance. With licensure requirements, states can establish educational standards for brokers and agents, create operating rules and standards, and punish brokers and agents who abuse the public and other professionals. States can also insist that brokers are either bonded or compelled to contribute to a recovery fund so that consumers can be compensated if a broker acts illegally.

7. *All fees and commissions are negotiable.* There is no rule, anywhere, requiring that brokers charge a particular fee for their services.

Importance. There are no standard, usual, regular or normal fees. If one broker will not negotiate fees, buyers and sellers have a right to go elsewhere. Conversely, brokers may not be restrained from offering their services at any price they elect to charge.

8. *Broker interests must be disclosed.* A broker cannot buy, sell, appraise or rent property for himself, or his immediate family, without full written disclosure.

Importance. Brokers and agents have a marketplace advantage by virtue of their training, experience, and education. Stating that someone has a license gives notice to everyone else in a transaction that they are dealing with a professional. In the case of appraisals, brokers or agents cannot appraise a property in which they have a current or potential interest, or where a fee is based on results.

9. *Discrimination is illegal.* Federal and state laws make discrimination illegal and create substantial penalties for those who discriminate. Beginning with the Civil Rights Act of 1866, federal, state and local laws have prohibited many forms of housing bias, including discrimination based on race, religion, national origin, gender, marital status, physical condition and age.

Importance. From the broker's perspective, who buys, sells or rents property is irrelevant. The greatest possible access to the housing market suggests the greatest number of deals, something every broker should welcome.

10. *You need a license to collect.* There is no rule that prevents individuals from buying or selling without a broker, but there are laws that prohibit individuals from acting as brokers. To prevent unlicensed individuals from competing, fees for brokerage services are simply uncollectable without a license. In other words, if Gentler helps Woods sell his home and then asks for a fee, the owner owes nothing if Gentler is unlicensed.

Importance. There is money to be made in brokerage, but being "in brokerage" requires a license.

A TEST

"This class is just a starting point," said Hoffman. "We don't have enough time to review more ideas or to study the ones we've covered in greater detail. Once you leave here your real education will begin, and hopefully that education will not be a costly experience for either you or your clients.

"The next step is to see if you can apply the ideas presented in this course. The upcoming state exam is a two-hour test with 75 questions, some relating to specific state regulations but most concerning general real estate matters. So that you'll have some idea of what to expect, here are 10 sample questions. Pick the *best* answer for each problem.

1. Agent Martin finds a buyer for the Prentiss home but at closing Prentiss refuses to pay a commission.
   A. Martin should sue Prentiss for the commission.
   B. Martin should accept a smaller fee and not waste more time with Prentiss.
   C. Martin should get a commission from the buyers.
   D. All of the above.
   E. None of the above.

2. Seller Larrabee wants to market his property but will not sell to blacks, Catholics or Jews. A broker should:
   A. Take the listing.
   B. Take the listing and ignore Larrabee's instructions because they are discriminatory.
   C. Take the listing but make a point of introducing the property to blacks, Catholics and Jews.
   D. Not take the listing.

3. Agent Franks tried to sell the Powell house but after three months was not successful. Powell withdrew the listing but later sent Franks a $500 check for her time and effort. Franks should:
   A. Return the check.
   B. Cash the check.
   C. Ask for a bigger check.
   D. Give the check to her broker.

4. In a typical residential transaction, who is most likely to have an agency relationship?
   A. The property owner and an agent.
   B. The property owner and a listing broker.
   C. The property owner and a buyer.
   D. The property owner and a selling broker.

5. Broker Cain has a trust account with $100,000 in security deposits for client properties and no settlements scheduled for 60 days. Cain can:

A. Withdraw an amount equal to his commission from his escrow account before closing.
B. Withdraw money only at closing.
C. Take money from the escrow account to operate his business.
D. Withdraw money only with permission of a buyer and seller.

6. *A salesperson can do which of the following in his own name?*
A. List property for others.
B. Sell property for others.
C. Both A and B.
D. Neither A or B.

7. *Seller Allen is unhappy with broker Myles. In the usual case, Allen can:*
A. Discontinue the listing contract because he is dissatisfied.
B. Reduce any commission owed to Myles.
C. Negotiate with Myles to end the listing agreement.
D. Ignore his listing agreement with Myles and hire another broker.

8. *Which of the following claims may be true:*
A. We sell homes faster than any broker in town.
B. We can get more for your home than any other broker.
C. We sell more homes than any broker in the county.
D. We charge the standard fee for our services.

9. *To get the best possible appraisal, owner Williams can:*
A. Fix up his property before the appraiser visits.
B. Agree to pay a higher fee for a higher appraisal.
C. Agree to list his property with the appraiser.
D. Have the property appraised by broker Mason, a co-owner.

10. *Agency can be created with:*
A. A legal and binding contract developed by a knowledgeable real estate attorney.
B. A broker's actions.
C. A broker's statements.
D. An individual's belief that a broker is acting as his or her agent.
E. All of the above.

ANSWERS AND EXPLANATIONS

Real estate exams show how theory can be applied in practical situations. The questions asked may seem strange or obscure at first, but they each relate to important principles.

1. Agent Martin finds a buyer for the Prentiss home but at closing Prentiss refuses to pay the commission.
ANSWER: E. NONE OF THE ABOVE. Martin is an agent, not a broker, and so has no direct relationship with owner Prentiss. Rather than suing Martin on his own, accepting a smaller commission, or trying to get the buyers to cover his fee, Martin must have his broker handle the problem.

2. Seller Larrabee wants to market his property but will not sell to blacks, Catholics or Jews. A broker should:
ANSWER: D. NOT TAKE THE LISTING. Larrabee wants a broker who is willing to act illegally. Brokers who hope to remain both solvent and in business should avoid such sellers.

3. Agent Franks tried to sell the Powell house but after three months was not successful. Powell withdrew the listing but later sent Franks a $500 check for her time and effort. Franks should:
ANSWER: D. GIVE THE CHECK TO HER BROKER. Franks, an agent, has no right to accept a check from anyone except her supervising broker.

4. In a typical residential transaction, who is most likely to have an agency relationship?
ANSWER: B. THE PROPERTY OWNER AND A LISTING BROKER. An agent has no direct relationship with a client, and surely the buyer is not trying to get the best possible deal for a seller. A selling broker—a broker who locates a buyer—is a subagent operating under the authority of the listing broker. The seller and the listing broker have a direct agency relationship.

5. Broker Cain has a trust account with $100,000 in security deposits for client properties and no settlements scheduled for 60 days. Cain can:
ANSWER: D. WITHDRAW MONEY ONLY WITH PERMISSION OF A BUYER AND SELLER. If a deal goes through a deposit will be released at closing, but only because buyer and seller agree. Money cannot be taken from an escrow prior to settlement

because a deal may fail if financing is unavailable, a structural inspection is unsatisfactory, or for some other reason. Deposit money held in escrow by a broker can only be released with the mutual consent of both buyer and seller. If they do not agree to release the money, then it's typically turned over to a court.

6. *A salesperson can do which of the following in his own name?*

ANSWER: D. NEITHER A OR B. A salesperson can neither list nor sell property without a broker.

7. *Seller Allen is unhappy with broker Myles. In the usual case Allen can:*

ANSWER: C. NEGOTIATE WITH MYLES TO END THE LISTING AGREEMENT. A listing agreement is a contract and the terms are binding on both broker and client. Unless there is a clause allowing a client to withdraw unilaterally, an unhappy seller must work out a suitable arrangement with a broker.

8. *Which of the following claims may be true:*

ANSWER: C. WE SELL MORE HOMES THAN ANY BROKER IN THE COUNTY. All properties, buyers, sellers, and deals are different, so there is no way to prove that a home can be sold faster or for more money because one broker is selected and not another. All fees are negotiable, so a "standard" fee does not exist. It may be objectively true that one firm sells more properties than all other companies in a given geographic area.

9. *To get the best possible appraisal, owner Williams can:*

ANSWER: A. FIX UP HIS PROPERTY BEFORE THE APPRAISER VISITS. An appraiser cannot accept a fee based on results or conduct an appraisal with the hope of future gain, in this case a listing. Since an appraisal is supposed to be independent and neutral, by definition a co-owner cannot objectively value property in which he has an interest.

10. *Agency can be created with:*

ANSWER: E. ALL OF THE ABOVE. Agency can be created by contracts, acts, statements, or the failure to act or make statements. To clarify relationships, brokers in more than 30 states automatically provide disclosure statements to would-be customers.

3
Listing Agreements

"Up to now," said Hoffman, "we've talked about what you can do and what you can't do. You can't be in real estate without understanding how the game is played, but once the rules are known we can get on to the one subject that concerns everyone: getting paid for your work.

"To make money when selling homes, your broker has to act as an agent for a principal. To show that he works for a principal—and to collect a fee—your broker needs a special piece of paper called a "listing" agreement.

"A listing is nothing more than an employment contract that defines the broker's job. It shows that the broker is an agent, that the broker has certain rights, and that when the broker meets the precise requirements outlined in the listing agreement, he is entitled to full payment for his services.

"As an agent working under the broker's authority," Hoffman continued, "you are entitled to some portion of the commission. How much is a matter that you and your broker must negotiate."

In the usual case, sellers hire residential brokers to find a buyer "ready, willing and able" to purchase property at a particular price and terms. If the Conklin house is listed at $185,-000, and broker Eldridge finds a buyer who makes an offer for $185,000 and has the financial capacity to purchase the property, then Eldridge has done his job.

The "usual" case, however, is rarely so simple. Suppose buyer Gittens offers $185,000 but as part of his offer demands that Conklin re-paint the living room. Unless Conklin offered to re-paint the living room in the listing agreement, Gittens's offer does not meet the precise terms of his contract with the broker.

Or, Gittens can offer $184,999. It's surely a good offer but it doesn't meet the listing agreement's exact terms. To deal with alternative offers, listing agreements are typically written so that a commission is due once an owner accepts any price and terms, even if they vary from the original listing contract.

What happens if Gittens offers Conklin $185,000, meets all the conditions of the listing agreement, has money to buy the property, and then owner Conklin decides not to sell? In this scenario broker Eldridge found a buyer ready, willing and able to purchase the property, fulfilled his employment contract, and is owed a commission.

What happens if the buyer changes his or her mind and decides not to go through with the deal? Sale agreements normally say that if a buyer will not complete a contract then the deposit will be lost. If the deposit is forfeited, then it is usually divided between the seller and the broker. If the broker is owed $5,000 for a commission and there is a $12,000 deposit, the seller and broker will generally divide the first $10,000 so that each receives $5,000. Any money remaining is then given to the seller.

Around the country various listing forms are specially designed to meet state and local requirements. Such forms typically show a property's street address (1401 Norton Street) as well as the legal address (Lot 2, Block 6, Ford Subdivision). They must have a starting date, a termination date, a commission arrangement, and a specific offering price.

In addition, well-written listing agreements are likely to contain a number of other important clauses.

Advertising. A broker will want the right to advertise the property, including the right to place a sign on the front lawn.

Commission. How much is the broker to be paid? Residential brokers are commonly paid a percentage of the sale price, but it is also possible to be paid by the project or on an hourly rate.

Deposit. When making an offer, buyers normally put down a cash deposit to demonstrate their intent to go through with the deal. A listing contract can show the minimum amount that a seller will accept as evidence of good faith.

Description. What is being sold in terms of bedrooms, baths, parking, kitchens, and other features? A full description defines the property and provides valuable sales information. Listing agreements are often printed on a single sheet of paper along with a lengthy checklist of features.

Financing. Is the seller willing to provide (take back) financing for a would-be buyer? If so, how much and under what terms? Take-back clauses depend—or should depend—on the seller's satisfaction with the buyer's credit.

Fixtures. What is being offered with the property? The stove, furnace, or central air-conditioning system? Sure. But what about the washer and dryer? They can be moved, so are they included in the sale or not? If offered in the listing agreement, the broker can include the washer and dryer as well as other items when describing what is for sale.

Lock Box. Lock boxes are devices that hold house keys and can be attached to doors. Brokers have a common key that opens such boxes and thus gives them access to a property. A lock box clause generally gives brokers permission to use a lock box and limits their liability if lock box keys are used to enter a home illegally.

Non-discrimination. The property will be made available to any interested buyer, regardless of race, creed, national origin, religion, or other factors irrelevant to a real estate sale.

Ownership. A listing will show whether the property offered for sale is a condominium, a cooperative, or fee-simple real estate. The form of ownership is important because different types of ownership represent more rights than others and are therefore considered more desirable.

Points. A listing form may ask how many "points" a seller is willing to pay. One point is equal to 1 percent of the value of the mortgage, say $1,000 on a $100,000 loan. Points are paid to lenders at closing to hold down interest costs for *borrowers,* so homeowners are usually loath to pay such fees.

Protection Period. Listing forms routinely contain a clause saying that if someone sees the property during the listing period but buys within a certain time after the listing ends— say 45 days—then the listing broker is entitled to a fee. If the property is listed with another broker then the protection period should end automatically.

Special Conditions. A listing can contain amendments to meet the precise needs of both sellers and brokers. There might be an instruction not to show the property on Saturdays or to beware of the dog. Or, settlement may be contingent on the seller's ability to buy and close on a new home. Another common condition is to sell something in "as is" condition, perhaps because the outdoor light on the front lawn doesn't work. There is no limit to the number of special conditions that can be included in a listing agreement.

EXCLUSIVE VERSUS NON-EXCLUSIVE

From the broker's standpoint, the most important features of a listing agreement are the rights received from a seller. How much authority has the broker obtained? Will he or she be the only broker selling the home, or will competing brokers be involved?

Open Listing. With an "open" or "general" listing a broker has the authority to sell a property but little else. An owner can sell by himself and not pay a brokerage fee, or an owner can hire 20 brokers simultaneously with open listings.

Suppose owner Grenoble doesn't want to list exclusively with any particular broker, but broker Lane says he has a buyer. In this situation, Grenoble can agree to an open listing with Lane. If Lane's customer buys the property, Lane can collect a fee. If Lane's buyer doesn't like the property, Grenoble will keep selling.

With open listings it is important to assure that such contracts not only have a termination date, but that they end automatically if the property is sold, listed exclusively with a broker, or taken off the market.

Exclusive Agency Agreement. Rather than an open listing, brokers greatly prefer "exclusive agency" arrangements. The attraction of an exclusive agency deal (at least for brokers) is that during the listing period the seller agrees to work with only one broker.

With an exclusive agency agreement the owner still has the right to sell directly and without paying a fee, but this right can create conflicts. If broker Fuentes has an exclusive agency agreement to sell the Nash home and Nash finds a buyer, can we be certain that Nash found the buyer directly? Is it possible that Fuentes' signs and advertisements alerted the buyer to the property?

If Fuentes' marketing "introduced" the buyer to the property, did it set off an *unbroken chain of events* that lead to the sale? If there was an unbroken chain, was Fuentes the *procuring cause* of sale and therefore entitled to a commission even though the buyer dealt only with Nash the owner?

Exclusive agency agreements are more attractive to brokers than open listing contracts because they at least allow the broker to have a competitive advantage. Still, exclusive agency agreements leave an area of ambiguity. With exclusive agency contracts it is possible for a broker to spend time, talent, and money marketing a property only to find that the seller has legitimately made a direct sale and that no commission is due.

Exclusive-Right-to-Sell Agreements. For brokers the best possible arrangement is the exclusive-right-to-sell agreement. The beauty of exclusive-right-to-sell contracts is that many issues disappear with this arrangement. Simply stated, if a property is sold during the listing period—whether by the

broker, the owner, the owner's brother, or another broker—
the broker who lists is the broker who collects.

Net Listings. Banned in many states, net listings allow a broker to be paid the difference between a benchmark price and
a sales price. For example, a seller might want $100,000 for
a property and agree to pay a broker anything above that
amount. If the property is actually worth $150,000 then the
broker will receive a $50,000 selling fee. Sellers rely on
brokers for pricing and marketing advice, so net listings can
allow brokers to take advantage of ignorant sellers, not a
good arrangement in a system where client interests are
supposed to come first.

Oral Listings. In theory it is possible to create an oral listing,
a situation where a seller says sell and then pays a fee if the
broker succeeds. If, somewhere, brokers are allowed to take
oral listings, the inherent problem with such arrangements
is that they are unenforceable.

If a listing is oral, then what is the listing price? What is the
rate of commission? When did the contract begin and when
does it end? Both seller and broker may agree, but if they
don't, then how can a broker collect? If the broker says the
list price was $100,000 but the seller says, no, it was $125,000,
who is right?

BUYER LISTINGS

The listing agreements above all secure a broker's right to *sell*
property. But brokers can act also as agents for purchasers, an
arrangement known generally as buyer brokerage, buyer's brokerage, or buyer agency.

With a buyer agency agreement, a purchaser will outline
basic interests such as price, location (say a particular subdivision or street), size, condition, and specific financial terms
(Smith will only buy if a seller pays all closing costs). As with
property listings, a buyer brokerage agreement must have a
beginning date and a termination date, and it must show the
broker's fee.

Buyer agency listings parallel traditional seller listing agreements. The various buyer agency listings are:

Open Listing. Both the broker and the buyer look for a property. If the broker finds one purchased by the buyer, a commission is due. If the buyer finds a property independently, no fee is earned. The buyer can have open buyer brokerage agreements with as many brokers as he or she wants.

Exclusive Agency. With this form of listing the purchaser agrees to work with only one broker during the listing period. The buyer cannot hire another broker during the listing period (unless he wants to pay two brokerage fees), but he still has the right to look independently. If a property is found without the broker's help, no fee is due.

Exclusive Right to Buy. In this case the contract will provide that if a purchaser buys within the listing period then a fee will be due, whether the property is located by the purchaser or the broker.

Net Listing. Net listings between brokers and sellers are commonly banned, but suppose a broker says, "Look, the Hartwell property is on the market for $200,000. If I can get it for less, would you pay me 25 percent of the difference?"

As long as the buyer does not purchase a broker's listing, net arrangements seem far more plausible for purchasers than for sellers because with buyers, the broker is not setting the sale price.

Oral Listings. It may be possible to create an oral buyer agency agreement but why bother? All the problems that make oral listings unattractive for brokers and sellers apply to brokers and purchasers. Oral listings, as the expression goes, are worth the paper they're written on.

MULTIPLE LISTING SYSTEMS (MLS)

One of the most important selling tools in real estate is nothing more than an organized collection of information known as a multiple listing system (MLS). Showing past sales and current listings, an MLS allows brokers to price property, determine market trends and locate suitable properties for would-be buyers.

An MLS can also be something more than a database. Many MLS networks, *but not all,* create an instant and immediate *subagency* option when a property is entered into the system.

Suppose broker Klein lists the Roswell property. Klein enters his listing into the local MLS and by doing so he automatically makes a "blanket offer of subagency." With a blanket offer of subagency, any broker who is a system member now has the right to show the Roswell property.

Klein made an "offer" of subagency, so other member brokers may accept or reject the offer. In the usual case there is no reason for member brokers to reject the offer unless they represent buyers.

Although an MLS may seem fairly simple and straightforward, the agency/subagency system has an enormous impact on the real estate marketplace.

The ability to convey property information quickly to large numbers of brokers clearly benefits homeowners. But an MLS system also does something else. It rewards member brokers with important competitive advantages.

For the cost of an MLS membership, perhaps $500, a broker can gain immediate access to all listed properties, a billion-dollar inventory in many systems. This means that to be successful in real estate, a fledgling broker doesn't need vast amounts of start-up capital. Combine a small office with MLS membership, and a new broker—or any broker—can have immediate access to most local properties at the smallest possible cost. Compare start-up costs in real estate with virtually any other business and it's easy to see why every community has large numbers of brokerage firms.

MLS networks are also important because they are used not only to market real estate, they are employed to market real estate services. Individual property owners cannot belong, and in many states only brokers affiliated with particular professional groups may join. An MLS is exclusive, and whatever the values of exclusivity, if homeowners want to use an MLS they need to hire a broker.

Before a property can be entered into an MLS it must first be listed, but not any arrangement is acceptable. Most MLS networks use only *exclusive-right-to-sell* contracts. The result is that when many or most local listings are entered into an MLS, member brokers have a stronger marketplace position than non-members, non-brokers and owners.

MLS networks have changed in recent years, however. In a growing number of systems, all brokers may join rather than just those affiliated with selected professional groups.

Another important change concerns listing arrangements. Rather than an exclusive-right-to-sell agreement or nothing, many systems now accept exclusive agency agreements. With such contracts homeowners can list property with a broker and have the property entered into an MLS, but still retain the right to sell it independently and without a fee.

4

Adventures in the Real World

In a typical year more than 200,000 people become licensed real estate agents, a vast army filled with entrepreneurship, energy, and hope, each looking for success in a field where admission is easy but prosperity is elusive.

Most will never see the promised land of big deals and fat checks. Real estate, as they will discover, is more complex than it appears, a business where the fundamentals can be learned in a few hours while the refinements can fill a lifetime.

How does it really work? There's a big difference between real estate as taught in classrooms and real estate as practiced in the streets, something Wilson discovered a few weeks after he took his licensure exam.

The letter from the state government was polite and to the point. In so many words it said, "Congratulations. You're an agent, so go out there, help people buy and sell, and just have a great time. Oh yes, when you sign up with a broker please send $125 so we can issue your official license."

Wilson was elated. With a license he could be an agent and as an agent he could make deals. All he had to do was find a broker.

There were hundreds of brokers listed in the local phone book, so in an absolute sense finding a broker was not a problem. Locating a broker who could help Wilson make big money was less simple, but Wilson eventually went with Woodside Realty.

Woodside stood out because it had offices throughout the area, belonged to the MLS, advertised frequently, and had a school to train new agents. Woodside also had superstar agents who probably cleared $200,000 a year, the best lure ever devised to attract new agents.

Wilson met with Jane Cooper, the manager of the local Woodside office, and they agreed that Wilson could keep his full-time job but that he would attend training sessions with Woodside two nights a week. Cooper would work with him on his first several deals and any commissions he generated would be split 50/50 with the company.

HOURS AND TAXES

In Cooper's eyes, Wilson represents little risk and much potential. Wilson is a "center of influence," someone with friends, neighbors, and co-workers who might want to use his services. Wilson is also a potential customer. Even if he never brought a single deal to the company, he is a homeowner and the probability is that one day he will move.

Cooper has told Wilson that real estate "isn't a 9-to-5 job," an expression that is literally true. Agents work days, nights, weekends, and holidays—what they don't do is work as employees. Instead, real estate agents are typically "independent contractors," a description with important tax implications.

If Wilson is hired as an "employee" then Woodside will have to pay Social Security and unemployment taxes, but as an independent contractor Wilson is responsible for paying his own state and local taxes. He also must pay Social Security taxes at a far higher rate than employees because there is no employer to share the bill. As for unemployment insurance, forget it. Wilson is not an employee and therefore cannot become unemployed.

Forget, as well, company contributions for health insurance, pensions, or profit sharing. Wilson can pay for a health plan and he can set aside money for IRA and Keogh accounts, but there is no employer to subsidize such costs.

THE GREETING RITUAL

Around the office Wilson saw that many agents picked up leads by taking "floor time"—manning office phones and dealing with walk-in prospects who came by to ask about properties.

The catch is that not all contacts are fair game. The way it works with many brokerage offices is that if a caller or walk-in asks about a property, the agent who responds has a claim to that prospect. If a caller or walk-in asks for an agent by name, or asks for the lister of a particular property, then the prospect "belongs" to the named agent.

At stake in the greeting process can be commissions worth thousands of dollars. If a prospect is interested in a property listed by Wilson but doesn't ask for Wilson, then whoever answers the prospect's questions is deemed to be "working" with the would-be buyer.

One exception to the greeting ritual is the manager. Whenever a potential buyer or seller asks for Cooper, she meets with the prospect but then assigns the prospect to an agent. With this system Cooper never competes with her agents and each agent has a fair chance to get new business.

FARMING

Within Woodside there are agents who specialize in listings while others prefer to work mostly with buyers. The business process at Woodside is simple: use the MLS exclusive-right-to-sell listing form, require a 6-percent commission, and show both in-house listings and those of other brokers.

Since other brokers use the same agreements and want the same fee, how do Woodside agents snare clients?

The firm itself helps by advertising extensively and by holding regular homebuying and homeselling seminars. The free seminars provide usable information, and always conclude with informal clusters where consumers can ask questions. A Woodside agent heads each cluster and it is at the clusters that business cards are distributed and names collected.

Beside seminars and ads, Woodside agents use many strategies to find new business.

Connie Larkin, for example, has made floor-time a science. Larkin figures that if she straddles the lines of communication, then anyone who calls or walks through the front door is naturally her prospect. She logs many hours of floor time and the secretary refers many potential prospects to her as a result.

Willie "the Mailman" Beaumont sends out 3,500 newsletters each month to every home in the Coral Heights neighborhood. He fills his letter with community news, recipes, school information, as well as the latest sales and listings. Concentrating in one area—a "farm" in real estate lingo—Beaumont naturally comes to mind when anyone in the neighborhood wants to sell.

When the town was founded, Clark Daniels built the first bar and later the first bank. His descendant, Missy Daniels, lists only the largest homes in the city, properties frequently owned by her friends, relatives, and members of the exclusive Founders Club.

Charlie Cason defines another listing strategy: joining. Cason belongs to every group, civic organization, and community association in town. Everyone knows good old Charlie, and good old Charlie brings in many listings.

LISTING WARS

A few weeks after Wilson began working at Woodside he met a would-be seller through Cooper. The seller, Clausen, lived within a mile of Wilson.

Like all sellers, Clausen wanted a quick sale at the highest possible price. Woodside had sold many homes in Clausen's neighborhood, so Wilson assured Clausen that the firm could do a good job.

"That's fine," said Clausen on the phone. "Can you come over here Tuesday night at 7:30. I want to hear how you'll sell this place, what you'll charge, and how much you think I can get. I'm speaking to several agents so give me some paper to work with."

Tuesday night Wilson was ready. He had assembled a list of all sales during the past year in Clausen's neighborhood, listed all houses now on the market, and pulled together brochures written for past Woodside listings in the area. The house, Wilson thought, would sell for $160,000.

Clausen thought otherwise.

"You've done good work, Mr. Wilson, but you're too conservative. Another broker says I should list this place at $172,000 and sell for $165,000. Even if he's wrong, by starting at a higher price I have room to bargain. In the worst case I can always accept $160,000. I appreciate your efforts, but your price is too low."

Discouraged but not finished, Wilson tried again with yet another would-be seller, Mr. Bailey. This time around, he made his lists, looked at other homes in the neighborhood, and came up with a $140,000 price for Bailey's property.

"I think we should list this property at $145,900," said Wilson. "We probably won't get that price, but at least we'll have room to negotiate. Anything from $140,000 or higher is a good price."

"Speaking of negotiation," said Bailey, "what about that fee of yours. If I got $146,000 I wouldn't mind paying 6 percent, but you're saying I'll probably get less. If I can take less, what about you?"

Wilson didn't have the authority to negotiate a lower fee, but he did make one point to Bailey.

"If the property sells for less than $145,900 my fee automatically drops because it's based on the sale price. Like you, I want the best possible price for the property. If the commission rate declines and the property sells for less than the listing price, then I lose twice."

Bailey wasn't thrilled with Wilson's answer but at least it was not unreasonable. As long as fees are tied to selling prices, then the interests of brokers and sellers are united. Bailey suggested that Wilson come by later in the week.

The big appointment was Thursday night and Wilson was excited. His first listing! Not bad after just a few weeks in the business. Remembering his experience with Clausen, Wilson decided to bring help. He brought Cooper.

Everyone sat around Bailey's dining room table, drank coffee, and got down to business.

Did Bailey want to list? Yes.

Would Bailey agree to the MLS listing that everyone else uses? Not exactly.

Bailey had bought and sold property before and he knew—although neither Wilson nor Cooper ever mentioned the term—that the proposed agreement was an exclusive-right-to-sell contract. Bailey wanted several changes.

"This form says that I should state how many points I'll pay at closing. If I agree to pay 1 point now, then I've agreed in advance to a concession without even seeing the buyer's offer. For purposes of the listing, I won't agree to pay any points. If we get a good offer I may change my mind.

"The other change we need to make concerns this business of exclusivity. I've talked to several people about this property and if you want the listing, then let's agree that if I sell to Tom Finch, Harley Kline or Mandy Simmons, there will be no fee. The rest of the world is exclusively yours."

Cooper nodded yes and Wilson brought out the magical form. Everything was going well, there would be a 90-day listing, and the deal was about to be completed when Cooper spoke up.

"Mr. Bailey we've agreed to several concessions we don't normally make, and we have one for you. This is Thursday night, the 6th. We'd like the agreement to start Sunday the 9th, at 9:01 A.M. That would give us more time to print materials and to take other steps to sell the property. We can still have an open house Sunday. Would that be okay?"

Bailey agreed and the deed was done. Leaving Bailey's house Wilson had just one question: why did Cooper want the listing period to begin Sunday?

"It gives us extra time to prepare materials for the listing," said Cooper.

"There is also the matter of MLS rules. In our MLS, we must enter every listing within 24 hours after it becomes effective. Our listing with Bailey begins Sunday at 9:01 A.M. which means we don't have to enter the property until Monday morning.

"We know we have the listing but we can't show the house until Sunday. Other brokers don't know that the property will be listed, so we can tell our agents and our other offices in advance and get a jump on the competition. With any luck, we'll have the place listed and sold before other brokers know what happened."

PHONE LINES

At this point Wilson has an exclusive-right-to-sell listing agreement, an open house scheduled, an ad running in the Sunday paper, plus Woodside agents who know about his listing. All he needs is a buyer.

The big day begins with little interest and few calls, perhaps because Wilson arrived at the office at 8 A.M., not exactly prime time. About 10 A.M. the phones start to ring and the secretary is at her post, transferring calls to agents, taking messages, and answering questions.

Wilson looks at the front desk and realizes that although other agents didn't list the property, they may get a piece of the commission. If someone doesn't ask for Wilson by name, or if someone fails to ask for the lister of Bailey's property, the secretary may refer them to an agent on floor duty. Once referred, they become prospects of whoever gets the call.

In the morning Wilson gets several calls, takes down names and phone numbers, and then suggests that people meet him at the property since it will be open at 1 P.M. All seems to go well until Idlewood, a local broker, calls.

Idlewood had seen the ad and wants to know if he can show the house to a prospect when it is open.

Wilson was unsure. The property was not in the MLS and therefore no offer of subagency had been made. He went to Cooper.

"Before we have a listing agreement we're adversaries with whoever is selling," said Cooper.

"We want the best listing and the highest commission and sellers want something else. Once that listing is in effect, the rules change. We're not adversaries any longer, we're agents, and the client's interests come first. In our case, that listing started at 9:01 A.M. and if someone had called at 9:02 to show the property, we would make reasonable arrangements.

"Sure we'd rather sell without another broker, but if another broker can interest someone in the property, then our job is to grab the offer. Remember the rule, we must show a property when it's in the client's benefit to do so.

Wilson couldn't think of any reason to ban Idlewood, but he also didn't understand how Idlewood could get cooperation because the property was not in the MLS.

"When we enter a property into our MLS an automatic offer of subagency is made to all members," said Cooper. "Nothing says we can't offer subagency to brokers who are not MLS members. There's also nothing that says we can't offer subagency before a property is placed in the MLS or even if a property is never entered into an MLS.

"Tell Mr. Idlewood that we are delighted to offer subagency, that there is a 3-percent co-op fee, and if he wants to show any of our other properties we'd be happy to set up appointments. If he needs something in writing, we can either fax him a form or you can give it to him at the open house."

McNeil was another broker who called. He knew the property and wanted to know if he could "register" a couple, the Dovers, with whom he had been working. McNeil wanted to show them the property but couldn't because he too was sitting at an open house. By "registering" a prospect, McNeil is asking Woodside to recognize that he has "introduced" the Dovers to the property and that if they are interested in buying, he will receive a co-op fee.

Wilson again spoke to Cooper.

"We have to be practical. The time will come when you are working with some buyers, you're holding an open house or have to be out of town, and the buyers want to see a property listed by McNeil. You'll want the same courtesy, so tell McNeil he can register his clients if he gives us their full names. Also find out what they like and what they need. That information may help us."

Just before he was about to leave, still another call came in, this one from an agent named Hopkins. Hopkins wanted to see the house, was interested, and wanted to know if he could receive a credit equal to the 3-percent co-op fee if he bought it.

"In this case," said Cooper, "we have an agent who may want to act as a purchaser. He must disclose that he has a license.

"We also have an agent who, if he buys, wants to get part of the commission as a credit. That we cannot do. The problem is that Hopkins is an agent so we cannot credit any portion of the commission to him directly. We can credit his broker and then Hopkins and his broker can work out whatever arrangement they want."

SHOWTIME

Wilson was pleased that Bailey had prepared the property. There was soft music playing. The large collection of old furniture and boxes that had filled the basement had been carted away, so now the house seemed roomier.

Wilson placed his sign-in sheet on the dining room table and kept his phone log in a briefcase. A sign-in sheet would show who visited the property and when, valuable information if it was necessary to back-up his claim for a commission. In addition, the notebook could be used to record each phone call he made or received—who called (or who he called), the time, the topic, and how long the conversation lasted. It was dull stuff, but Wilson figured that without it his chances to keep a commission would be reduced.

Wilson had mapped out his strategy. If someone came he would walk them into the dining room, hand them a pen, and then have them sign his log as he went into the kitchen to get a brochure. In effect there was a trade. Sign the log and you get a brochure.

The general market was good and real estate prices where Wilson lived had been rising at 8 to 10 percent a year for several years. Housing was affordable and given this market, Wilson was not surprised to find several visitors per hour stopping by.

Most visitors were friendly, several were curious neighbors, and a few came with agents. Those who came with agents did not sign the log, instead the agent would leave a card with Wilson, a ploy that effectively concealed the buyer's name. Among those who showed up, however, were several interesting citizens.

Peterson went through the house twice, made copious notes and asked lots of questions. Pulling Wilson aside, he wanted to know if Bailey would accept $138,000.

Wilson had been trained for this moment.

"I know the seller will take $145,900," said Wilson. "I can't comment on any other price, but if you want to make an offer I'll be happy to sit down and we can write out the details."

"I don't want to work out the details, I want an answer," said Peterson. "Do you think the owner will take $138,000. Yes or no."

"I don't have an answer," said Wilson.

"You work with this guy. You listed the house. You mean you have no idea? I don't want to waste my time submitting an offer if you know it's bound to fail."

"My instructions are to offer the property for a specific price. I simply cannot suggest an alternative. If you want to see how Mr. Bailey might respond, then let me show him a written offer."

Another visitor was Beckworth, a buyer broker.

"I'm here with my client, Mr. Hamel, and if we make an offer on this property we would structure it so that my fee is paid by the seller. In other words, if you have a 6 percent listing, I'd get 3 percent. You need to tell me what you're getting as a commission, whether you would accept an offer from us, and if you would allow me to be there when you present the offer to Mr. Bailey"

Wilson had also been prepared for dealing with a buyer broker. At Woodside, buyer brokers were welcome, but information about relationships between Woodside and its clients was confidential.

"You're welcome to submit an offer," said Wilson. "As to your questions, let's go through them one at a time.

"You want to know our commission arrangement with Mr. Bailey. That's a private matter.

"You want to know if we will accept an offer that requires us to divide our commission with you, even though you are not a subagent and even though our commission might only be $1. It's up to Mr. Bailey to accept or reject any offer that comes in and for us to discuss with Mr. Bailey any aspect of the offer that concerns us and our listing agreement.

"You want to know if I will allow you to be present when I present the offer. Presenting an offer is a private matter, a form of consultation, between Woodside and our client. So no, you can't be present.

"Now, having gone through this little litany, submit an offer and let's see how the details can be worked out. If your buyer wants the property and my seller wants the sale, we're at least headed in the right direction."

In practice, Cooper had explained to Wilson that the most important matter was to get a written offer. If the seller wanted the deal, then Woodside would normally reduce its commission as an accommodation to the seller. The seller could then give a credit at closing to the buyer and the buyer, in turn, could pay his or her broker. What was not acceptable was a situation where a buyer broker interfered in the contractual relationship between Woodside and its clients.

Beckworth thanked Wilson and said he would discuss the matter with his client.

Another open house visitor was Thompson. Thompson signed the log but said he was working with a broker.

Buyers such as Thompson present major problems to brokers. Because Thompson doesn't understand how brokerage works, because the broker with whom Thompson is working never tried to "register" him, Thompson is blissfully unaware that Wilson can regard him as a prospect. The trick is to induce Thompson to make an offer without having a nasty battle over commissions. As Cooper had explained to Wilson, there are two ways to solve the problem.

"In a buyer's market, a time when homes are hard to sell, tell Thompson that you're elated that he has a broker and you welcome the broker's participation."

"In a seller's market when properties sell within days and multiple offers for a single home are common, tell Thompson to submit an offer. The details can be worked out later. If the seller wants Thompson's offer, that's fine.

"If Thompson's offer provides for a commission split with his broker, we can offer a referral fee to the broker, anything from dinner to a full co-op fee, depending on how well we negotiate and the other guy's position. Sometimes there's a real debate about how much should be paid and the matter must be arbitrated, but we can worry about that later."

After running into several brokers and many lookers at the open house, Wilson was relieved to find Harrison, a self-proclaimed buyer.

Harrison asked many questions. Would the seller hold some financing? Did the seller mind if closing was postponed a little bit? Would the seller agree to some repairs?

About an hour after Harrison left the open house he returned with an offer. Wilson was shocked. With just one open house he had sold his first property, a deal Bailey was sure to take since it was for the full asking price, $145,900.

Wilson called Cooper at the office and told her the good news. For some reason, Cooper seemed less than thrilled. Something was wrong but Cooper wouldn't discuss it over the phone. She wanted to see the offer before it was presented to Bailey and said she would be right over.

NO MONEY DOWN

At the end of the afternoon Wilson, Cooper and Bailey sat at the dining room table.

"We have received an offer for the full asking price but when you see the terms it will be clear that this is not the offer you want," said Cooper.

Bailey was not too pleased.

"What we have," Cooper continued, "is something that looks like a solid offer but is a mirage. Its a no-money-down, get-rich-quick scheme that assumes the seller is desperate, foolish or brain dead, the kind of thing you hear about on late night television. If you take this deal, the probability is that you'll lose and you'll lose badly."

Cooper then went through the major points found in Harrison's offer.

Harrison would get a $45,000 loan from Bailey to buy the property. In addition, Harrison would take over Bailey's five-year old FHA loan, a loan with $100,950 outstanding.

Bailey's loan would be secured with the house. However, Harrison reserved the right to subordinate the loan and to have the loan secured by alternative collateral selected by the purchaser.

"What does he mean 'subordinate the loan?' What is 'alternative collateral?'" asked Bailey.

"It means," said Cooper, "that Mr. Harrison wants the right to get additional financing on the property. If he does, then you are agreeing to allow another lender to collect his debt before your loan is repaid if the property is foreclosed. If the house is foreclosed, the other lender is paid in full and nothing remains to repay your $45,000 loan, that's too bad.

"As for substituting collateral, if you agree to that provision then Mr. Harrison can use something else to secure the loan instead of the house, say an old car. Then, if he defaults, you might be able to get the old car, but the loan will no longer be secured by your home."

"Also, our Mr. Harrison wants you to pay all closing costs,

there is no deposit with this offer, there is no downpayment, and Harrison wants the right to rent your house before settlement. Settlement can be as long as six months in the future.

"Mr. Bailey," said Cooper forcefully, "as a seller you have the right to accept any offer. If you accept this one we will ask that you sign a statement acknowledging that we advised you to reject this deal. We will also require you to pay our commission at closing, something that will be difficult since you are receiving no funds from the buyer.

"If the buyer walks away from the property, he has nothing to lose. You do. Since we are your agents, and since we are supposed to put your interests first, please deny us a commission and don't make a deal that is unreasonable, unnecessary, and unlikely to succeed. Let us find you a buyer who can make a downpayment, who can get financing, and who can make a deal so that when you sell the house, your financial connection is severed and you can buy a new home in peace."

A BUYER

A few days after the open house the office was still getting calls. Tuesday morning the entire office came out to tour the property, one of seven homes seen that day.

Wednesday afternoon an interesting call came in. The Cooks had seen the house Sunday and wanted to see it again. Could they make an appointment?

Wilson was elated. Why would someone want to see a house twice if they didn't like it?

There was no other agent involved with the Cooks so that solved the problem of cooperating with another broker or splitting a fee with a Woodside agent. The Cooks had seen the house, so they at least knew what it looked like. Thursday night. Seven P.M. Yes, that's fine.

At the appointed hour Wilson showed up in his best suit and finest persona. The listing had been fun, but this was better. A deal! His first one and it only took a week to sell.

The Cooks were a young couple buying their first home. Mom and Dad would help with a down payment and co-sign all loan documents, so financing was not an issue. Pricing and condition were.

"You want $145,900 for this property and while it's in great shape, other well-maintained homes in the area sell for $138,000 or $139,000. We can offer $138,500, but no more."

"The property is listed at $145,900," said Wilson. "If you offer too little the property may be bought by someone else. You saw how many people we had at the open house. There's a lot of interest in this home. The more you come up in price, the better your chances of getting the property. I can't reveal the details, but I can say that the owner has already rejected one written offer and you can guess why."

After a little more haggling back and forth a price of $140,250 was offered by the Cooks along with a $5,000 deposit. They also wanted several concessions.

"We want the washer and dryer included in the sale," Mr. Cook said. "And we want the deal to depend on financing. If we can't get a loan at the right terms, forget it, there's no sale and we want our deposit refunded."

"Well," said Wilson, "I must ask Mr. Bailey about the washer and dryer. Since they are not in the listing agreement I can't offer them with the property. As to a financial contingency, that's built into the offer form."

"We read what's built-in," said Mrs. Cook. "The problem is the language you have here is not good from our perspective. The form says that we have a deal if we can find 10 percent money. But later on it also says that we agree to accept 'such rates and terms as may be available at closing' and that means we may have to choose between a very high interest rate and losing our deposit. We don't want to be in that position.

"The 10-percent rate is irrelevant the way this thing is written," she continued. "Let's knock out the tricky language and say that we will agree to an interest rate not to exceed 10 percent and if 10 percent or less is not available then the deal is off."

The Cooks were also unhappy with the tax provision.

"The little form says that purchasers agree to pay all transfer taxes. That's 1 percent of the purchase price. Is there any law that requires us to pay these taxes, or is it just part of the form?"

Wilson acknowledged that it was part of the form and added that "buyers always pay transfer tax, it's tradition."

"Call us untraditional," said Mr. Cook. "But we want our offer to split the transfer taxes."

FINANCIAL STATEMENT

"Our next step is to complete a financial disclosure form," said Wilson. "It will just take a few minutes to fill out the standard form Woodside uses."

"We really don't want to complete your form," Mrs. Cook responded. "Our finances are a matter for us and the lender to consider. You represent the seller. If we tell you everything our negotiating position will be diminished."

"I see the issue a little differently," said Wilson. "If Bailey accepts your offer he is essentially pulling his property off the market while you look for financing. Meantime, who pays the mortgage? Who pays the taxes? Bailey has to know that you have the assets and credit necessary to buy a home in this price range."

As Wilson and the Cooks haggled back and forth, a compromise emerged. The Cooks agreed to complete the form but to provide only minimal information. For example, they described their cash on hand as "$20,000+" a statement that was literally true and yet sufficiently vague to hide the total cash they had available.

PRESENTATION

After Wilson finished with the Cooks he called Cooper and told her what happened.

"What you have is an offer and the Cook's deposit, what we in the real estate business call 'consideration.' To create a contract you need an offer, consideration, and acceptance, so you haven't got a deal. Yet."

At the property Wilson and Cooper presented the offer, the financial qualification sheet, and a copy of the $5,000 deposit check. After going over each point, Wilson waited for Bailey's response.

"What this tells us," said Bailey, "is that our pricing is on target. We need to straighten out some of these conditions. I really would like to get $145,900 for my property, but we both know that is unlikely. Besides, if I pay for half the transfer taxes, I lose more than $700. If I give up the washer and dryer, I'll need a new set when I move and that will cost me at least $800.

"Also, I said I wanted 10 percent down to seal an agreement and all we have here is $5,000. That's a big check, but it's about one-third of the $14,000 or so that I should get according to the listing agreement.

"We've only had the property listed a week and it's entirely possible that we'll get more offers," he continued. "We can't guarantee that more offers will come in, but why not come back to the buyers with a counter-offer?"

"Be aware that if you make a counter-offer the original offer is dead," advised Cooper.

"The buyers can walk away and not even respond. That's the chance we're taking."

Bailey decided to take a chance. He wouldn't pay taxes and he wanted a $300 credit for the washer and dryer—not as much as they were worth, but less than it would cost the buyers to get new equipment.

A PACKAGE DEAL

The Cooks didn't seem particularly surprised by Bailey's response.

"It's an interesting offer but we've found a house on Pine Street. The price is $2,000 less, the yard is bigger, and the seller will pay taxes. Thank Mr. Bailey, we like his house, but the only way we would agree to his terms is if we can buy with a lower price."

Wilson thanked the Cooks as graciously as he could and then called Cooper.

"Remember what I said about offer and acceptance?" asked the manager. "Well, the Cooks offered and Bailey rejected. That's part of life. Just make certain to return the Cooks' uncashed deposit check, get a receipt for it, and tell Bailey what happened. Tomorrow we start again and perhaps Bailey will be more flexible."

REALITY SETS IN

Wilson had been lucky. Two offers in a week for the Bailey property. What happened next was grim. Few phone calls, few agents making appointments, and little traffic at open houses.

It wasn't just that the Bailey property was not selling, the general market had slowed. The problem was August. Many people were on vacation. As for Bailey, the offer made by the Cooks was looking better with each passing week of inactivity.

Enter the Turners. They had seen the Bailey house with agent Carlson at Richmark Realty. The Turners liked the property, liked the location, and wanted to make an offer. The deal: $139,500 for the house with a $5,000 deposit. The sale would be financed with the Turners putting down $14,000 and obtaining a loan for $125,500. In essence, a deal with 90 percent financing and no points for Bailey to pay.

The deal also had three hurdles.

First, Carlson—probably the top agent in the local MLS— had inserted a clause requiring the Turners to apply for financing within 10 days and show that they could qualify for a loan.

This clause really had two provisions. First, it forced the Turners to promptly apply for financing. If they didn't apply for a loan, then possibly they could lose their deposit.

The clause also said that the Turners had to get a letter showing that they qualified for a loan. This generally means that a loan officer supplies what is called a "hand-holding" letter, which says that based on the information supplied by the purchasers they appear to qualify for financing. The letter will also say that verifications and an appraisal will be required; therefore the letter is not an absolute financing commitment. In other words, the loan officer is saying, hey, we met these people, they seem alright, but we need to investigate further before writing a check.

Second, the Turners also didn't like the contract's financing provisions. Either they got a fixed-rate loan with 10-percent interest or less *and* 2 points or less, or the deal was off. By specifying a limit on both points and interest, they avoided a potential problem where a lender has a low interest rate that conforms to the sales contract but then charges many points.

Third, the Turners wanted a structural inspection.

"We'll hire the structural inspector," said Mr. Turner, "and if the inspection is not satisfactory to us, the deal is off and we'll get our money back immediately."

Wilson was glad the buyers had brought up a structural inspection. It protected their interests and it also protected his position as well. It would be tough to claim that Wilson, Carlson or Bailey had hidden something when an outside inspector had examined the property.

When Bailey saw the Wilson offer he seemed relieved. The apparent price was not as high as the offer from the Cooks, but then the Turners would pay all transfer taxes. Also, Bailey had mellowed with time. He was less certain about prices and demand than when the property was first listed. He accepted the offer.

INSPECTIONS

Most real estate contracts require an inspection to show that a house is free and clear of termites and other wood—boring insects. If a house is infested it must be treated. If a house has been damaged by insects, then the sellers may be required to make full repairs, some repairs, or no repairs.

Structural inspections are relatively new but have become increasingly common. With a structural inspection, someone selected and paid by the purchaser examines the house. The inspector can be anyone but many of the best inspectors are affiliated with a group called ASHI, the American Society of Home Inspectors.

The Turner inspection clause included several important conditions:

- The Turners would find their own inspector. This was terrific because it meant the buyers were not relying on either Wilson or Carlson to suggest an expert.
- The Turners would pay for the inspection. This made seller Bailey happy.
- The inspection would be held within 10 calendar days.
- The inspection must be satisfactory to the Turners. The term "satisfactory," as Wilson knew, was a loaded expression that hid an important value. If the house was structurally perfect, it could still be "unsatisfactory" to the Turners ("It's perfect. Gee, that's too bad. We really wanted a house that was in poor condition so we could fix it up").

  By making the deal depend on a "satisfactory" inspection, the Turners could always end the deal by merely saying the examination was not acceptable.
- If the inspection was unsatisfactory, the deal was finished

and the Turners would get their deposit back immediately.

What the Turners had really created was an option. No one else could buy the property for at least 10 days, so the Turners effectively had an option to buy or not to buy without cost and without competition from other potential buyers.

A few days later Wilson met with the Turners, Carlson, and the inspector, Haines. Haines, who carried enough equipment to dismantle the house, proceeded to test every appliance, socket, pipe, and valve he could find, and he found them all. He used a ladder to check the roof and he examined both the basement and the attic. He peered into the furnace, took the electric service box apart, worked the thermostat, and produced a checklist that ran 12 pages long, promising as he left to deliver a full written commentary within 24 hours.

The next day Carlson called Wilson with the verdict. The Turners liked the house but would not regard the inspection as satisfactory unless Bailey replaced aluminum wiring that connected several kitchen outlets to the electrical service box. The cost: about $600.

Wilson told Bailey the news and Bailey, with great distaste, agreed.

As he spoke to Bailey Wilson realized that not only did the structural inspection create an option for the Turners, it also allowed them to re-open negotiations. Had they simply produced a lower offer up front, Wilson was not certain Bailey would have accepted it. By breaking the offer into two parts, the Turners first obtained an option on the house and then perfected the deal.

Wilson was learning.

MORTGAGES

Carlson was the selling agent, so he worked with the Turners to obtain financing. They checked with more than 20 lenders by phone, asking about rates, terms, and programs. Finally, they agreed to apply with Mr. Abbott at Concrete Savings and Loan.

The Turners met with Abbott and spent nearly two hours completing a loan application. Abbott promised that they would know within two weeks if their loan had been approved, subject only to an appraisal of the property.

The Turners could have been qualified within an hour with some lenders but they found that lenders who offered quickie loan programs also required higher rates—about half a percent higher on the average. While it doesn't seem like a lot, on a $125,000 loan the difference between 9.75 percent and 10.25 percent interest is $46.18 a month, a total of $5,542 if the loan is outstanding just 10 years.

The Turners also picked Abbott for another reason: he clearly explained how each loan worked, showed all the charges, and provided the "annual percentage rate" (APR) for each loan program. The APR is important because it shows a true interest rate, one that includes the cost of points as well as the apparent interest rate. For example, a 9.75-percent loan with 1 point has an APR of 9.87 percent.

CLOSING

Eight weeks after Bailey agreed to sell it was time for closing. If a contract can be viewed as a script, then settlement is simply the play itself where everyone follows their lines.

At settlement the seller gets cash and the buyer gets property. The seller's lender, if any, will be paid off unless the loan is being assumed. Taxes, title insurance, and the cost of closing will be paid.

In addition, money may be set aside in an "escrow" or trust account if it is necessary to complete certain work. In Bailey's case, if the aluminum wiring had not been replaced before closing, the settlement provider would have held $600 in escrow to cover the repair work.

Also at closing copies of the termite inspection are given to each party, and the buyer brings in a paid-up fire, theft, and liability insurance policy.

Bailey expects to get paid at closing, a "wet" settlement, but in many cases payment is deferred a few days until the deal is recorded in local property records.

Brokers are also paid at closing. In the case of the Bailey

property, there was a 6-percent commission and a sale worth $139,500, so the brokerage fee was $8,370. Of this amount, Woodside received $4,185 and Richmark Realty where Carlson worked received the other $4,185.

DIVIDING THE COMMISSION

At closing Woodside received a $4,185 check from the attorney who conducted closing. Cooper and Wilson met to divide the money, a 50/50 split which meant that Wilson received a check for $2,092.50.

From listing to sale four months had elapsed and a review of his records showed that between listing, showing, negotiating, financing and closing the deal, Wilson spent 74 hours working on the Bailey property. Dividing his fee by the hours worked, he was getting $28.28 per hour.

Figured over a 40-hour work week, Wilson was earning almost $59,000 a year, less costs for medical coverage, sick leave, pension deposits, and Social Security payments.

The problem was that Wilson did not earn $28.28 every hour. He earned a particular hourly rate for the Bailey deal, but he might earn more or less with other properties. In the best case he could sell a home within a few hours. In the worst situation he wouldn't sell anything.

What Wilson saw is that rather than easy money, brokerage is an entrepreneurial activity with no guarantees. Big commissions happen, but in the typical deal with the typical agent, fortune does not await.

As to Woodside Realty, they took in $4,185 and paid out $2,092.50 to Wilson. The remaining $2,092.50—an amount known generally as the "company dollar" in the real estate business—had to cover advertising the Bailey property, office rent, MLS fees, phone bills, taxes, secretarial time, Cooper's salary as a manager, Cooper's bonus on the work generated by her office, legal fees, accounting costs, and all the other expenses required to stay in business.

With any luck (and it would take luck) Woodside's *pre-tax* profit probably amounted to 6 percent of the entire commission, the industry average for mid-sized firms, or $251.10 for the Bailey sale. Seen another way, on the sale of an item worth

$139,500, Woodside's profit margin was ultimately .0018 percent.

Richmark Realty, the selling broker, also took in $4,185 but Richmark's expenses were different from Woodside. Richmark has all the operating costs faced by Woodside except advertising for the Bailey property. Richmark, however, had to pay Carlson, and Carlson was a superstar agent who received 85 percent of each commission dollar earned. Richmark took in $4,185 and promptly gave $3,557.25 to Carlson. Richmark's profit was that it kept Carlson happy and a happy Carlson brought both attention and agents to the firm.

TALK WITH A SUPERSTAR

A few days after the Bailey settlement Carlson called and invited Wilson to lunch.

Carlson was something of a mythical figure among local agents. A good agent might list and sell properties worth several million dollars, but Carlson had handled transactions worth $33 million in the past year. Entire firms did less business than Carlson, so an invitation from the area's number one agent was not to be ignored.

Lunch was an informal affair with polite conversation until Carlson started to talk about the Bailey deal.

"I thought you did a good job," said Carlson. "I know the Bailey property was your first sale but you obviously have a future in real estate. If you don't mind my asking, tell me about working at Woodside."

Wilson explained his 50/50 deal with Woodside and the training and support they offered. He was happy to be there, said Wilson.

"That's a fair deal for an entry-level agent," Carlson responded.

"In my case I get 85 percent of everything I take in and I take in a lot. You know that last year I had listings and sales worth $33 million and this year I should do better."

"How do you handle so much business?" asked Wilson. "I know how many hours it took with the Bailey deal and I just can't imagine where you get the raw physical time to deal with so many people."

Pouring more coffee, Carlson waited for a moment before answering.

"It's really simple, I don't put in as many hours per sale as you do.

"There are two sides to real estate when you represent sellers. You can list houses and you can bring in buyers as a selling agent. I do both.

"Each month I send out 25,000 pieces of mail. It's my biography. If I meet someone, they're on the list. If I list a house, the owners are on the list. If someone signs a log at an open house, they're on the list. I don't care who they are, what they earn, or how I met them. After this lunch you'll be on the list and once you're on, you're on forever.

"You know why I mail so much? I keep my name in front of people. The people I reach have friends, relatives, co-workers. Everybody knows Carlson the agent. I get a lot of business.

"In fact, I get too much business. I get better than a 100 calls a day. At home, at the office, in the car. I'm attached to the phone. I can't deal with so many people, so I have associates. I have two full-time secretaries. I have agents who show houses. I have agents who chauffeur buyers. They each get someone to work with and each time I close a deal where they have handled the buyer or seller, I get a fee and they get 60 percent of whatever I take in.

"If you ever want to do more business, I've created a machine that generates hundreds of leads every week. Think about it."

Wilson thought about it and realized that if 11 people—Carlson and his 10 associates—did business worth $33 million, then each was doing an average of $3 million yearly.

To get that business Carlson was sending out 25,000 pieces of mail per month. If his cost for printing and mailing averaged out to 40 cents per item, then his yearly mailing cost was $120,000.

Also, Carlson may handle transactions worth $33 million, but some portion of those sales are co-op deals, just like the Bailey sale. In that case the property was worth $139,500 but Woodside listed and Carlson—through Richmark—sold it.

If half of Carlson's deals are co-ops, and if a typical deal has a 6-percent fee, then Carlson really averages 4.5 percent on his transactions. On sales of $33 million, Richmark is taking in $1,485,000. Of that amount, 15 percent ($222,750) is going to Richmark while Carlson receives $1,262,225.

Of the money he receives, Carlson gives 60 percent to his agents, that's a total of $757,350, or about $75,000 each. He keeps $504,900 for himself. Subtracting $120,000 for mailing and $50,000 for secretarial help, leaves $334,900.

Carlson's agents are doing well. The world is not filled with too many jobs that pay $75,000 for people who don't operate, litigate, manufacture, or manage. As to Carlson's income, many corporate executives make less.

As Wilson thought about Carlson he had one question.

"Why do you work for Richmark? You can surely set up your own office, use the same system, and produce the same results, only this time without losing 15 percent to a supervising broker?"

"But your real question is why don't I dump Richmark and maximize my profits? If I run my own office and play administrator there's less time for brokerage and brokerage is what I do best.

"And one other thing. I'm the best agent in town. I make more than Richmark so why should I take a pay cut to become a broker?"

PART II
Where We're Going

No one doubts or denies that the real estate business is more competitive today then even five years ago, but increased competition does not mean that all changes are now in place. Instead, it is more appropriate to suggest that the real estate revolution has only begun, that we are merely at the start of a process rather than at the finish.

What further changes will real estate see?

- Some patterns that have begun to show up recently will become more widespread. Buyer agency is an example.
- New forms of competition and practice will emerge. Mixed-fee realty supermarkets, as one illustration, will be part of the future in many communities.
- Some old practices will continue. Self-selling will surely be with us, but probably in a somewhat different form than we have seen in the past.
- External events will greatly affect the industry. A surplus of lawyers as well as a chance to supply mortgage services will create new opportunities for brokers.

The following chapters outline specific areas where change is likely to occur, and suggest how such changes will influence real estate practices and consumer choices nationwide.

5

Discount Brokerage

Armed with a capitalist's zeal and a pilgrim's innocence I decided in 1978 to launch my very own real estate company. Founded on the bedrock proposition that a new broker needed something to stand out in a crowded field, I felt the best way to gain clients was with lower rates, a perspective not greeted with vast enthusiasm by some in the local real estate community.

Undaunted, I plunged ahead. Instead of charging a 6-percent fee, I offered my services on the following basis: 4 percent of the first $100,000 and 2 percent of the sale price above $100,000. If a property sold for $150,000, my fee was $5,000 versus $9,000 for a 6 percenter.

Given a choice I would have greatly preferred to charge more money, but I couldn't compete with other brokers on the basis of experience, size, or longevity. Only cash was left and I was certain that with my discounted fee system I could generate business.

I not only wanted clients, I wanted something else as well. I was giving a discount and in return I wanted clients with the right properties. If a home didn't show well, if the location was poor, or if the price was too high, then clearly someone charging a 6-percent fee should have the honor of marketing that property.

To get the right houses and to promote my company I embarked on a letter-writing campaign. I started with a particular street where homes sold for about $150,000 (an above-average price in the late 1970s, but not enough for a mansion or estate), drove by, marked down the houses that seemed most salable, and then sent a letter to each homeowner introducing both myself and my services.

From the street I knew location would not be a problem and by driving around and looking at exterior areas I could at least make a basic judgment about condition. All I needed were sellers with a reasonable sense of pricing and I was in business. Fortunately my letters attracted attention and soon I was listing and selling properties.

Although it was easy to get business as a discounter, the concept was not without problems. One difficulty was cooperation with other brokers. Even among those who were interested in showing my properties, low commissions were a barrier. Take my fee, say $5,000 on a $150,000 deal, divide it in half and a cooperating broker was making $2,500. If a buyer was brought in by an agent, then the selling agent and selling broker were each likely to receive $1,250—not much compared to what they could get with conventional co-op fees.

To get around the co-op problem I changed tactics and went to an uneven split system. With a property worth $150,000 my system worked this way.

- If I sold the house directly I would get a 4-percent commission, $6,000 in this example.
- If I listed the property but another broker brought in a purchaser, then the seller paid a 5-percent fee. I received 2 percent ($3,000), while the selling broker received 3 percent ($4,500). The effect of this arrangement was to make my listings competitive with homes listed at 6 percent.

Although the split-fee system did attract other brokers, I was unable to assemble a vast army of agents. This was not surprising because my commissions were low; cut in half they were tiny. Agents could do better elsewhere and they did.

Not having many agents had attractions. Administration was held to a minimum, and for the most part there were no commissions to split because I alone listed and sold properties.

The down side to an agent-less brokerage was that my ability to handle business was limited. If I showed two houses every other Sunday—one from 11 to 2 and another from 3 to 6—I could list a grand total of four homes at any one time.

Still, as an independent broker with few costs, four listings at a time could be very productive. If a home typically required 60 days to sell, and if four homes could be listed at a time, then I could potentially handle 24 houses a year. If each house was worth $150,000, then my sales volume for the year could be $3.6 million. If I had an equal number of direct sales at 4 percent and co-op deals at 2 percent, then a typical fee would be 3 percent. On sales of $3.6 million, I could generate a gross income worth as much as $108,000.

As a discounter I offered the same package of services that traditional brokers offered. I advertised, held open houses, assisted with negotiations, and did much of the work required to bring a deal to closing. What made discounting practical, however, is that my economics differed radically when compared with full-service brokers.

I didn't need to make as much per sale as traditional brokers because I had far-lower operating costs. My listing expenses—in terms of both time and money—were essentially zero. People came to me because at the time I was one of the only brokers, perhaps the *only* broker, who openly offered discounts in my community.

In addition, because I was a small broker who listed and sold properties directly, there was no agent with whom I had to split fees. Whatever I collected at closing was both my gross commission and my net commission.

To see the difference between my service and that of a traditional broker, consider what would happen if a home worth $150,000 was sold.

- If the property was marketed by a traditional broker with a 6-percent fee, the owner would pay a commission worth $9,000. The deal was likely to involve an agent, so both the agent and the broker would probably receive $4,500.
- If I sold the same house directly with a 4-percent commission, I would earn $6,000—a higher net amount than traditional brokers received after they split fees with an agent.
- If I listed a house and a buyer was found with an agent who

worked for a cooperating broker, then the fee arrangement would look this way: I would receive $3,000 (2 percent) and the cooperating broker would get $4,500 (3 percent). If the co-op fee was divided between broker and agent, then each would receive $2,250. Once again, I would have a higher net payment than a traditional broker.

- If a house was listed by a traditional broker and I brought in a purchaser, then the 6-percent commission would be split 50/50. I would receive $4,500 and the traditional broker would receive $4,500. The traditional broker would then split the fee with an agent, but I wouldn't because I generally had no agent with whom to split.

- Only if a traditional broker both listed and sold a property would he or she come out ahead. And while some independent brokers were able to list and sell houses by themselves, it didn't happen that often.

What's the bottom line?

First, as deals become less complex, when fewer agents and brokers are involved in a given transaction, it then becomes possible to provide a full package of services at a lower cost.

Second, selling real estate services at a lower price does not necessarily mean less broker income.

Discounting worked well and had great potential—at least until the market soured. The prime rate topped 20 percent in 1980 and 1981 and with much to sell and few buyers, my interests—like those of many people in real estate at the time—turned elsewhere.

Several trends now in place—greater price competition, cheap computers, and the growing use of home offices—will make full-service discounting a more powerful competitive force in the 1990s. If large numbers of brokers elect to work at home, do a few deals each year, and compete on the basis of price, they will take listings from traditional firms. Put enough discounters into the marketplace and suddenly the aggregate number of listings they handle can be substantial.

6

Services Unbundled:
The Menu Approach

Restaurants have always allowed diners to purchase either complete meals or to buy à la carte. Pick the full dinner and you get the owner's view of what a complete meal should include, but if you're not so hungry, then it can make sense to choose from the à la carte list. You might pay more per item but the final cost for the evening is often lower.

Like complete meals, real estate services are typically purchased as a single package. With traditional brokers you pay one price and get an all-inclusive package, everything from advertising to negotiation.

Instead of selling a traditional package of services, however, there are brokers who use the à la carte approach and allow clients to buy only the services they want. Known as "flat-fee" or "set-free" brokers, such firms are fully licensed, often affiliated with local MLS networks, and able to provide everything from signs to a complete package of services.

By their mere existence set-fee brokers raise an interesting question. Who says that every aspect of a real estate sale necessarily requires the use of a broker? If sellers do some of the work, shouldn't marketing costs decline?

Instead of tying fees to sale prices, flat-fee brokers charge by the service. For sellers who want several services but not a full package, the obvious lure is lower overall marketing costs. If brokerage fees in a given community typically total 6-percent and Robinson can sell a $150,000 house by paying broker Knutsen a fixed sum, say $3,500 instead of a 6-percent commission, then Robinson is ahead.

In addition to lower marketing costs, set-fee brokerage offers two less visible benefits: control of the sale and marketplace leverage.

When traditional brokers work for owners there is often an effort to separate buyers and sellers. Buyers are told that they must communicate through brokers and sellers are advised to refer all inquiries to their brokers. In this system brokers become a filter, often protecting sellers, acting as a shield against harassing and time-consuming buyers, and frequently presenting a stronger position than sellers might be able to project.

On the down side, filters have been known to clog and when that happens problems can arise. Maybe an owner has not been kept abreast of the latest developments. Perhaps an agent in good faith is not making the best possible case for a seller.

Some owners—those with good selling and negotiating skills—may not want to insulate themselves from buyers. For them direct contact with purchasers, and control of the selling process that direct contact creates, is a better choice.

In the example above with seller Robinson we created a situation where a fee was reduced from $9,000 to $3,500. The difference between the two fees is not only $5,500, it may also be marketplace leverage.

If Robinson sells with a 6-percent commission, then a $150,-000 sale will produce a net price of $141,000 ($150,000 less $9,000). If he pays marketing costs of only $3,500, then a $150,-000 deal will create a net price of $146,500 ($150,000 less $3,500).

We can now see what happens if Robinson's house sells for $150,000. But what if the market turns sour? What happens if Robinson's house can only be sold for $145,000?

With the 6-percent fee Robinson will now receive just $136,-300 ($145,000 less 6 percent, or $8,700). If he sells with a flat-fee broker, Robinson will receive $141,500 ($145,000 less $3,500). In this example $141,500 is more than Robinson would have received even if a traditional broker had sold his home for $150,000.

There is another example to consider. Suppose Robinson simply wants a quick sale. His marketing costs with a set-fee broker can be lower than sellers who use full-fee firms so he has additional bargaining room.

For example, if homes similar to Robinson's are selling for $150,000 but marketing times often exceed six months, he might elect to reduce his price to get a quicker sale. If he drops his price to $147,500, he will still net $144,000 ($147,500 less $3,500)—more than sellers paying 6-percent fees and marketing their homes for $150,000.

Some buyers will understand that Robinson's marketing costs differ from sellers who use traditional brokers and will attempt to share the benefit of lower marketing costs. Who wins—Robinson or a buyer—will depend on the marketplace.

- If the market is strong then Robinson can sell at full price and pocket any commission money he saves.
- If the market favors neither buyers nor sellers, then Robinson may take a somewhat lower price to move his house quickly, in effect losing some of the money he saved on brokerage costs.
- If the market favors buyers then Robinson may be forced to sell at a steep discount and give up all his potential savings.

If the economics of set-fee selling potentially benefit both buyers and sellers, what about brokers?

Given an equal number of transactions, smaller fees per sale, and similar selling prices, a set-fee broker will generate less income than a full-service competitor. Gross income, however, does not address the question of bottom-line profitability.

In a $150,000 transaction a full-fee, full-service broker charging 6 percent will collect $9,000—unless the sale is a co-op deal with another broker. If half of all transactions involve broker cooperation, then there is a 50/50 chance that a broker selling $150,000 properties will collect from $4,500 to $9,000, or a $6,750 average.

From his $6,750 commission, a broker must pay an agent. If the agent receives 50 percent, the broker now has $3,375 left for office costs, advertising, legal fees, and other expenses.

In the above example, the set-fee broker charged $3,500 to market the Robinson property. There is no co-op fee, so the broker keeps the entire $3,500. From his $3,500, the broker must pay an agent and with a typical 50/50 split, the broker has $1,750 remaining to pay office costs, advertising, legal fees and other expenses similar to those of his full-fee brethren.

With fewer dollars coming in, how does the set-fee broker stay in business? The answer is volume.

The set-fee broker can handle more properties per agent because agents are not showing houses or driving would-be purchasers around town. With more listings per agent, the flat-fee broker can prosper with fewer agents and a smaller office than traditional competitors.

So far it seems that set-fee brokerage produces lower selling costs and attractive economics for brokers. Given such advantages, why is set-fee brokerage such a small marketplace factor?

One reason surely involves history. In the past many set-fee brokers entered the marketplace with programs that required up-front, non-refundable payments whether properties sold or not. With such pricing, brokers could profit by listing homes rather than selling them, a strategy that can only attract owners in an environment where sales are assured. Slow times invariably hurt brokers who charge up-front fees and it doesn't take too many slow months to be out of business.

A second factor is volume. When markets slow down and the number of transactions declines, flat-fee brokers can be in trouble as ad costs and other expenses per listing mount. Full-fee brokers, with fewer sales but bigger margins, are more likely to survive.

A third reason that set-fee brokers do not dominate the marketplace concerns sellers. Simply stated, not every owner can effectively represent his or her own interests, and not every owner wants to.

A final barrier is pricing. Set-fee brokers may charge less, but a lower price is not always a bargain.

In the example with Robinson we created a scenario where the owner found a purchaser and paid a total brokerage fee of just $3,500. But what if Robinson could not find a purchaser directly? Suppose Robinson wanted his property entered into the local MLS system.

To attract broker interest Robinson must offer a co-op fee, say 3 percent of the sale price. If the property sells for $150,000, he will owe $3,500 to the set-fee broker plus $4,500 ($150,000 × 3 percent) to the selling broker, a total of $8,000—just $1,000 less than a traditional broker might charge.

Robinson might actually save even less than $1,000 if he wants the flat-fee broker to show his property. If there is a $500 showing fee, then Robinson in the *best* circumstances is ahead only $500, not enough to attract many sellers.

The nature of set-fee brokerage is such that most users are unlikely to seek broker cooperation or to have brokers hold open houses. Instead, the best market for set-fee brokerage services is among self-sellers. Set-fee brokers offer many of the services that self-sellers want, and self-sellers—by definition—believe they have the capability to market their homes directly. Given the menu-type approach and lower costs offered by set-fee brokers, the fit between self-sellers and flat-fee brokers seems natural and appropriate.

As to competing with traditional brokers, it can be argued that whatever competition exists is largely superficial. Sellers who want the complete package offered by traditional brokers are unlikely to buy services à la carte. Sellers who want to show and sell by themselves are not likely to hire traditional brokers. What it means, in effect, is that traditional brokers and set-fee brokers both offer real estate services, but each serves a separate market.

7

100-Percent Commissions

Finding the boss in any business is usually a simple matter. The person with the corner office, the biggest salary, and the most perks is the maximum leader, the one individual who calls the shots and ultimately makes decisions.

In a real estate firm the unquestioned boss should be the broker. Not only is the broker's name likely to be on the front door, but brokers simply have more legal authority than agents. No agent can work without a broker, and no agent can deal directly with buyers and sellers.

If there was only one broker in the world it would be easy to see how he or she could have the upper hand when dealing with agents. But every market has many brokers, brokers need agents to boost sales, and brokers therefore compete for the best available agents.

How much brokers need agents is reflected in the most basic measure of all, fee splits. Entry-level agents may divide commissions on a 50/50 basis, but top agents can work remarkable deals, sometimes getting 80 percent or 90 percent of the commissions they generate.

Why would a broker give up so much of each commission dollar? If two homes are sold for $200,000 and both have a 6-percent fee, then why should the neophyte agent receive 50 percent of the fee while the top pro gets 90 percent? Surely a sale is a sale, so why the big difference in fees?

Brokers offer big splits to superstar agents because such agents bring in more than sales.

To see how this system works let's look at a superstar agent—we'll call him Mason—and see what happens when he lists and sells property worth $7.5 million in a single year. Imagine further that every deal produces a 6-percent fee and that not a single deal is a co-op with another broker. The fees in this situation total $450,000 and if Mason gets 90 percent he earns a total of $405,000. The broker keeps $45,000.

Mason has costs for licensure and auto expenses to deduct from his money. The broker pays for everything else including office space, secretarial support, phones, newspaper advertising, signs, equipment and one other important cost: a fat bottle of red ink every time Mason makes a deal.

In the strange world of real estate economics seemingly-absurd agent payments can make sense—at least in limited circumstances. Superstar agents like Mason provide visibility, activity, listings and sales. While superstars may not bring profits directly, they draw entry-level agents to the firm, and it is those agents with low commission splits that mean big broker profits.

If 10 agents list and sell properties worth $5 million, then with a 6-percent commission, fees worth $300,000 are generated. With a 50/50 split, the broker keeps $150,000, enough to cover expenses and produce a healthy profit margin.

Marketplace realities have shown that the superstar system works well for top agents and their brokers. Less clear is how well the system works for agents who are consistently productive but not superstars.

Suppose agent Lyons pulls down $75,000 a year. By the standards of the real estate industry (and most industries), he is doing well, but Lyons is not a superstar in the same league as agent Mason. If Lyons effectively splits 65/35 with his broker, then his transactions total $1.92 million per year, and his broker takes in $40,384. (Lyons, it should be pointed out, probably has a much higher transaction volume because we have not considered co-op deals.)

How can Lyons make more money? Until recently his choices were either to generate more business, demand a better commission split, join another firm, or become a broker and go out by himself.

Generating more business sounds good, but we have to assume that Lyons is already doing as much business as possible. In effect, he's reached his limit.

Negotiating a better commission split may not be feasible either. Lyons' broker knows—to the penny if he's smart—just how much revenue Lyons produces. Lyons is good, but he doesn't have the drawing power of a superstar and the margin he produces simply isn't good enough to justify a better split.

Joining another company is surely possible because other brokers would like to have his production. But their position is the same as Lyons' current broker–they can only pay so much for the dollars Lyons can bring in.

Lyons has been in the real estate business for many years, so he can easily take the courses needed and become a broker. Given his sales history, Lyons might generate more income but whether he sells or not he will also have greater expenses.

Given the pros and cons of the four choices above, the probability until recently is that Lyons would have stayed with his broker and worked on finding bigger deals or more deals. But a new choice is now available to Lyons, one that has profoundly influenced brokerage industry economics and relationships.

The 100-percent commission is not a new concept, but it is newly widespread and therefore a fresh consideration when looking into the relationship between brokers and agents.

With a 100-percent commission an agent goes out, makes deals, and—in most states—keeps everything he earns. Since an agent is still an agent, he must work under a broker's authority, a relationship that raises a question: If the agent gets 100 percent of the commission, what does the broker get?

Instead of a commission cut, the broker receives a monthly fee for the use of his authority and facilities, say $1,500.

If Lyons goes with a 100-percent broker and continues to do the same amount of business as before, $1.92 million, then with a 6-percent commission he will generate gross revenues of roughly $115,000. Subtract $18,000 (12 × $1,500) in annual office fees, and $97,000 remains.

With the 100-percent system, Lyons must also cover his direct advertising, perhaps $12,000 a year. So after office expenses and ad costs, Lyons is left with $85,000, about $10,000 more than he makes with his current broker.

Risks for Lyons include declining sales, higher advertising costs than anticipated, or a lengthy dry spell. No matter how much he makes, Lyons' $1,500-a-month expenses continue whether deals go through or not.

As to Lyons' conventional broker, he now has problems. If he raises the split he pays to Lyons, his revenues and profits decline. If Lyons leaves, then the conventional broker loses 100 percent of the income Lyons brought in each year.

Equally important, if the conventional broker does not keep Lyons he also loses the momentum, activity and vigor that Lyons brought to the company. Fewer signs, fewer deals, and fewer ads are not evidence of a successful business with which buyers and sellers want to associate.

The economics of 100-percent brokerage are entirely unlike those of traditional brokers. If Douglas is a 100-percent broker he has expenses for office space, equipment, franchise fees, secretarial help, and other typical business costs. Unlike a conventional broker, however, if sales are off one month or up the next, Douglas can at least count on steady income from his agents.

If Douglas has 15 agents each paying $1,500 a month he will generate a gross income of $270,000 a year. Douglas has no commissions to split with agents or payments to make for listing ads, so $270,000 is essentially net income merely for keeping the doors open. In addition, Douglas can also generate more income by listing and selling properties on his own.

Money alone is not going to lure Lyons or most other agents to a 100-percent broker. The 100-percenter must provide excellent facilities and services, otherwise productivity will drop.

The 100-percenter must also supervise his agents. That they are experienced and productive does not reduce his liability if they do something wrong. A broker who merely plays the rent-a-desk game with agents will soon be out of business.

Will Lyons jump to a new broker? Will Lyons' old broker give Lyons a better deal? There are no certain answers, but around the country a pattern has begun to emerge.

■ Productive agents such as Lyons are testing the waters with the new leverage created by growing numbers of 100-percent brokers.

- Commission splits are rising, company dollars are down and conventional brokers are being squeezed.
- By competing internally for top agents, 100-percent brokers have used an innovative strategy to capture sales and profits. They are, today, a major force in virtually every market nationwide.

What can conventional brokers do to hold operating margins and fend off 100-percent competitors?

One strategy surely involves lower commissions to less productive agents. They have no leverage and a 100-percent broker is not a practical option for them.

Raising client fees is an alternative, but not a practical one. Real estate competition is intense and the ability to charge 7 percent in a 6-percent market (or 8 percent in a 7-percent market) is virtually impossible.

Better deals for superstars such as Mason are neither possible nor probable. As it is now, between splits and perks brokers are effectively paying superstars more than 100 percent to stay with a company and there just isn't any more to give. In this situation, superstars are likely to continue with established firms.

The battle between conventional brokers and 100-percenters thus concerns productive agents such as Lyons who are not superstars but who consistently bring in deals. The 100-percenters have shown an ability to capture such agents and conventional brokers have responded with a willingness to pay better splits to top producers. No matter who wins the battle between traditional brokers and 100-percenters, successful agents who know how to play one side against the other have gained enormous leverage.

8

But Aren't Brokerage Services Free?

Real estate brokers lose income worth billions of dollars each year, a feat made possible because brokerage has always been a performance industry. Like the Indy 500, there is big money for those who make a sale, who come in first. Unlike Indy, coming in second or third yields only the three Zs—zip, zero, and zilch.

In a typical transaction there are listing brokers, selling brokers and a little-discussed third group, ghost brokers—individuals who might-have-been, could-have-been, should-have-been sharing a commission, but didn't.

Ghost brokers contribute time and attention worth billions of dollars to the homebuying system and while buyers and sellers should be grateful for such charity, the brokerage community impoverishes itself in the process.

Suppose West goes to a lawyer and asks about setting up a corporation—is it a good idea, what will it cost, what types of corporate structures are out there, and so on. An attorney—we'll call her Tydings—explores each question with West and at the end of 90 minutes presents a bill for $225.

West now has a bill. Whether he creates a corporation or not, he owes Tydings. If West subsequently goes to another attorney for corporate advice, Tydings at least has been compensated for her time and efforts.

With brokerage the system works differently. If West goes to broker Edwards to ask about buying an investment property—

is it a good idea, what will it cost, what types of properties are out there—Edwards will provide copious amounts of information.

Some of Edwards' comments will relate to specific properties, but much advice will concern general issues such as market conditions, investment strategies, prime locations, taxes, rental rates, lease requirements, and local zoning. After 90 minutes broker Edwards will receive a handshake and if West goes out the same day, uses Edwards' background information to his advantage, and buys property where West is not an agent or subagent, then Edwards doesn't get a dime.

Edwards' efforts can be seen as salesmanship, providing information with the hope of future gain. His efforts also can be viewed as an investment, risking time and information instead of capital.

Given that Edwards is risking his time by talking to West without assured compensation, just how much of a gamble is he taking?

A 1985 study by the National Association of Realtors shows that 55 percent of all buyers used one broker to find a home, situations where one customer plus one broker equals one commission.

The odds change, however, when the entire marketplace is considered. Forty-five percent of all buyers used at least two brokers. Specifically, the study showed that 23 percent of all buyers used two brokers, 14 percent used three brokers, 4 percent used four brokers, and a final 4 percent used five or more brokers.

The survey results lead to three conclusions:

First, for every 100 people who buy a home, at least 179 brokers are involved.

Second, for every 100 people who buy a home, at least seventy-nine selling brokers are likely to be frozen out.

Third, the survey does not say how many people use broker services *but do not buy a home.*

For broker West, marketplace realities confirm wallet-busting inefficiencies.

To create a simplified example, imagine that West acts only as a selling broker and does not list property. Suppose further that he earns $50,000 a year and that 55 percent of his contacts with actual buyers result in sales. If West can increase his efficiency to even 75 percent, his income will jump to $68,182 annually. Seen another way, by operating with typical levels of success there is more than $18,000 missing from his checking account each year.

One way West can generate extra cash is to reduce his unproductive time, to eliminate contacts with lookers, nonbuyers, procrastinators, and realty voyeurs. Unfortunately, prospective buyers do not wear signs that announce their intentions or broadcast their foibles, so West has little choice. He cannot ignore potential purchasers because there is no way to tell who will buy and who won't.

West operates at his peril if he elects to discourage those people who *seem* like time-wasters. Not only might he lose a bona fide customer, but coincidentally he might also turn away a variety of would-be purchasers including minorities, handicapped individuals and senior citizens. Refusing to deal with a particular individual can thus trigger concerns regarding unlawful discrimination.

West must deal with the public, but there is no rule saying his services must be free. He can charge for his time and training just like other professionals—at least in theory.

In practice West is going to have a miserable time. If he bills at $75 per hour to show houses, buyers will flock to other brokers who show homes without charge. If he lists a property and wants $25 every time a selling broker needs to show the house, selling brokers will simply take customers elsewhere.

While the outlook for brokers charging by the hour is generally poor, there are at least two situations where it can make sense for both brokers and clients to accept hourly bills.

First, if buyers have located a house and want to make an offer, they may elect to hire a broker to assist them in the negotiating process. Here the broker is not a finder who locates property, but a consultant who advises on such matters as past sales, current listings, home inspections, and payments for points, taxes, and closing.

Second, an owner who wants to sell independently can hire a broker for a few hours of consulting. In this situation there need not be a listing agreement in the usual sense because the broker is providing information, not representation.

If the broker is shrewd, however, he will use consulting payments to get additional business. It might work this way:

- The broker charges $100 an hour for his time.
- If the seller decides to list with the broker and the broker sells the property, then all hourly fees paid before closing will be a credit. In other words, if the brokerage fee is $5,000 and the seller has paid $400 for hourly consulting costs, then the broker is only owed $4,600 at settlement.

The attraction of billing by the hour is that money is earned, due and payable regardless of performance. If a supposed buyer spends two billable hours with a broker and elects not to purchase, the broker is not left empty-handed.

If brokers do bill by the hour, then what should they charge? Like commissions, hourly fees are a matter of negotiation, but at least brokers can look at their communities and see what other professionals charge. The hourly fees sought by lawyers and accountants are often a good index that shows what local people will pay for professional services.

9

Buyer Brokers

Let us imagine that after several years of marital bliss that two people—we'll call them Donald and Ivana—find themselves no longer in love.

Do they run off to the same lawyer? Not at all. They go into their separate corners and huddle with their separate attorneys.

Donald and Ivana have different lawyers because their interests conflict. They are smart enough to know that the attorney who represents one cannot also represent the other in an adversarial situation.

Buyers and sellers are like our fabled couple. Their interests differ, they have an adversarial relationship, and they know that the broker who represents one cannot represent a competing interest. Yet unlike couples facing divorce, buyers and sellers rarely seek separate representation. Instead one broker typically assists a seller, and if a deal involves two brokers then *both* commonly represent the homeowner.

We can see that the seller is well represented, but the other side of the table seems desolate and lonely. There, in regal isolation, sits the buyer, relying on limited skills and a gross shortage of experience to consummate the largest consumer purchase of all.

Although closing is the single place where the benefits of broker representation are seen most clearly, there are many points in a typical residential transaction where brokers have important roles.

- The broker helps establish a price when a property is first listed.
- The broker provides information showing how the property can be made more salable.
- The broker negotiates for the seller, trying always to get the best possible price and terms.
- Instead of helping the buyer make the strongest possible offer, the broker merely "transmits" the buyer's proposal to the seller. For example, if the buyer demands a roof inspection, the offer might say that the "purchaser reserves the right to inspect the roof." A mere roof inspection, as a broker knows, is not as good as an inspection which must be "satisfactory" to the purchaser. A right to inspect does not say that the deal is off and the purchaser's deposit will be refunded if the inspection is not "satisfactory."
- The broker supplies standardized contract forms with language that routinely favors the seller.

With so much of the marketplace favoring sellers, it is not surprising that buyers have increasingly begun to demand separate representation. Call it buyer brokerage, buyer agency or buyer representation, it is something that more purchasers than ever are now seeking. And interestingly enough, buyer representation has also begun to attract a growing number of brokers.

THE COMPETITIVE ANGLE

It is difficult to imagine any profession that maximizes profits while giving away 50 percent of its time, talent and energy, that has been the historic pattern within the real estate community. In a typical residential transaction, it is the seller who hires a broker, pays a brokerage commission, and is entitled to the broker's best efforts.

Yet for all the effort to attract business, "business" remains largely defined in terms of sellers. In effect, while seller dollars are hotly pursued, buyer dollars—which are equally spendable—are virtually ignored.

It is both appropriate and entirely ethical to represent sellers, but at the same time there is no reason to ignore the other side of the marketplace. Buyers need professional realty services and surely some purchasers will pay for a broker's experience, expertise and judgment. No less important, serving purchasers opens new and enticing professional opportunities that can lead to greater income and productivity for brokers.

THE BROKER'S PERSPECTIVE

Although buyer agents are only active in a small percentage of home sales nationwide, more and more brokers have begun to embrace the concept. What has caused the trend toward buyer representation is not public demand, but rather the business benefits that brokers can obtain by representing purchasers.

- Unlike the seller marketplace, there is less competition to represent purchasers; thus it's easier to attain marketplace distinction.
- Buyer representation is no less reasonable or ethical than seller advocacy.
- In a "buyer's market" it is better to represent those with bargaining power.
- Buyer representation is often more convenient and personally satisfying. For example, if Chrisfield asks his friend, broker Dumont, to find a house, Chrisfield is doing so because he trusts Dumont and recognizes his skills and abilities. Dumont, in turn, can fully and openly represent his friend. As a buyer representative, Dumont has no obligation to get the best price and terms for a seller he may not know.
- Buyer representation opens additional markets. As long as there is a buyer brokerage agreement, a broker can even collect a fee when a home is sold by a self-seller.
- Buyer representation may produce income even if no property is purchased! For instance, if a buyer hires a broker on an hourly fee, the broker is essentially a consultant paid by time instead of performance. If a deal doesn't go through and the broker spent five hours on the project, a fee is still earned, due and payable.
- Productivity will increase if purchasers must pay for pro-

fessional time. If a purchaser wants to go from house to house with broker Katz, that's okay if Katz is paid by the hour.

Knowing that the meter is running, few people waste a lawyer's time. In a similar fashion, if brokers charge for their time, then buyer loyalty will increase because purchasers will want to protect their investment.

- Separate representation for buyers and sellers clarifies broker responsibility. No one will wonder who a broker represents and therefore dual agency suits will decline.

Given many advantages to both purchasers and brokers, why has it taken so long for either buyers or brokers to become interested in the concept? The answer involves a complex mixture of tradition and money.

HOW IT WORKS

The system used by buyer brokers to represent purchasers is roughly similar to the concepts employed by brokers who sell property. In essence, buyer brokers attempt to "list" purchasers instead of houses.

We have seen that when brokers list real estate, they prefer "exclusive-right-to-sell" arrangements that virtually guarantee a commission if the broker can find a buyer during the listing term. Buyer brokers can list purchasers in a similar fashion with specialized contracts.

For example, broker Renwick can be hired as a finder to help Collins buy a certain type of property (perhaps a three-bedroom house), in a particular area (we'll call it Elm Park), within a specific period (say 60 days), at a specific price (say $150,000 or less). If a property that meets the listing terms is found, then Renwick will receive a commission established in advance (perhaps $4,500 in this situation).

We can modify the above agreement in many ways. If Collins wants a particular house, then the buyer agency contract might apply only to one specific property. Or, the agreement might provide that instead of a fee based on performance, Renwick will be paid by the hour as a consultant. In the usual case, a consulting agreement would be an "open" arrangement without exclusivity because the broker is being paid hourly.

We can even give Renwick two ways to earn a fee.

We might have Collins pay by the hour for approved work and thus guarantee some compensation. It could also be agreed that if a deal does go through, Renwick will receive a specific commission, say $4,500, *less* any hourly fees paid. For example, Renwick might put in 12 hours at $100 per hour. If no deal is made, then Collins owed $1,200. If a home is bought, then Collins owes $4,500. If Collins paid $1,200 to Renwick prior to settlement, then only $3,300 will be owed to the broker at closing ($4,500 less $1,200).

In a perfect world we want to pay a buyer broker with a specific fee (say $4,500) instead of a commission tied to the sales price (perhaps 3 percent of the sale price). If we agree to a percentage fee, then a broker can benefit by finding a more expensive property or by failing to negotiate strongly.

As a practical matter, however, the world is not perfect, most brokers are honorable, and many buyer representatives are paid on a percentage basis.

USING AN MLS

The buyer broker who belongs to an MLS system will use the service to find properties and compare price. Most MLS systems are based on an agency/subagency arrangement, so a buyer broker must use an MLS system with care.

The National Association of Realtor's *Handbook on Multiple Listing Policy* (Section 7.11) clearly states that buyer brokers have the right to use an MLS system and plainly require buyer brokers to give notice up front when they represent a purchaser.

While NAR policy allows buyer broker participation in an MLS system, not all courts agree. Rulings in a limited number of cases have prohibited the use of MLS systems by buyer brokers, preserving for a moment the view that only agents and subagents can belong to an MLS.

How an MLS system can be restricted is a mystery, somewhat like limiting libraries or classified advertising sections to right-handed readers. No agency activity is required to check MLS files for comparable prices, or to see which properties are currently available. In such situations MLS files are merely part of a database.

Denying buyer brokers access to MLS networks raises obvious questions and conflicts.

First, real estate licenses allow brokers to represent others in the sale *and* purchase of real estate. Since brokerage services are only available from those who hold realty licenses, it seems hard to imagine how brokers can be frozen out of an MLS merely because they are providing a lawful service.

Second, since MLS listings are likely to contain many if not most properties available in a particular community, purchasers who wish to use buyer brokers are denied access to many prospective properties.

Third, homeowners cannot maximize sale opportunities when would-be buyers are unable to obtain information about their properties. In effect, the rights of both buyers and sellers are restrained when buyer brokers are denied access to a local MLS.

Undoubtedly some soon-to-be-wealthy attorney will notice the gross unfairness of this situation and the few MLS networks that now restrict buyer brokers will change their ways.

WHO PAYS THE FEE?

On paper, at least, all the conditions are in place to make buyer representation attractive. Purchasers can clearly benefit from buyer brokerage. Brokers can gain new sources of revenue by charging purchasers. The need for brokers to represent *sellers* increases when buyer brokers become involved in a transaction because, of course, homeowners want their interests protected too.

So why, asks the cynic, if buyer brokerage is such a great and wonderful idea, don't we see purchasers clamoring for it? Why—if buyer brokerage is such a sure-fire income producer—don't we have entrepreneurial brokers lining up and offering their services to grateful purchasers?

The basic problem is money. Buyer brokers must be paid by someone and buyers rarely have the dollars necessary to underwrite the fees buyer brokers charge. Cash short buyers, in turn, set off a chain of events that ultimately leads to an unexpected source of buyer broker funding.

Look at a typical residential sale. The buyer enters the transaction with money and credit, the seller has a house. After the deal everything is reversed: the seller has the money and the buyer has the property. What the buyer does not have is additional cash to pay for a broker.

If marketplace representation is so important, then why doesn't the purchaser simply borrow more money to cover buyer brokerage fees?

Lenders have guidelines they use when making a mortgage, such items as how much of your income can be devoted to housing costs and how much debt you can afford. They also have rules about using mortgage funds to pay anything other than a very short list of housing costs. Among the items missing from that list are fees for buyer brokers.

The Department of Veterans Affairs, for example, prohibits payments to buyer brokers under VA loan programs. Department rules state that "brokerage or other charges shall not be made against a veteran for obtaining any guarantee or insurance," an expression that seems to discuss insurance brokers instead of real estate brokers, but a statement interpreted to mean that VA buyers cannot pay brokerage fees. Also, the Department refuses to pay buyer brokers because there is no provision that specifically provides that they can be paid.

With FHA financing, the rules are somewhat different. Finder's fees for brokers are permitted. The catch is that the combined cost of the home, closing expenses and a brokerage fee cannot exceed the property's appraised value.

FHA field offices can agree that a buyer's brokerage fee is a "customary" local charge, in which case it can be included among routine settlement costs. Considering that the volume of buyer brokerage deals in most areas is miniscule, it's hard to argue that something so rare can be defined as "customary."

Among private-sector lenders, there has been no rush to finance buyer-brokerage fees, a curious lack of interest among the lending fraternity.

Since lenders protect the sanctity of their loans with such contrivances as credit checks, title searches, termite inspections, and paid-up insurance policies, logic suggests that lenders would want to encourage buyer brokerage, a service designed to get better deals for purchasers and ultimately more security for lenders. Such logic, wherever it may be, has eluded the lending industry.

Let's see. Buyer's have a cash shortage and lenders do not

want to underwrite buyer brokerage fees. What about sellers?

Sellers can pay buyer brokerage fees, but homeowners are the very last people who should be underwriting such costs.

Sellers often pay a variety of buyer expenses, items such as points, settlement fees, and repairs. Seen as just another cost, there is no reason why sellers should be prohibited from paying buyer brokerage fees, if such payments can be negotiated within a deal.

The problem is that buyer brokerage fees are not simply another cost. A seller surely does not want to pay both a buyer brokerage fee *and* a full commission to the broker who listed the property. If the listing fee is 6 percent and the buyer broker wants 3 percent, then the seller's marketing costs will total 9 percent of the selling price.

Most sellers won't swallow that, and if they do, most lenders won't finance such deals. While seller concessions are allowed, a deal top-heavy with brokerage fees is not a good risk for lenders.

Perception is another problem that arises when buyer brokerage fees are paid by sellers. The buyer broker has entered the deal in order to get the best possible terms for the buyer, not an activity that rational sellers will joyously support.

It may be legal for the seller to write out a check for the buyer's representative, but by paying part or all of the buyer broker's fee, has the seller obtained a hidden or inadvertent concession from the purchaser's representative? Whatever the factual answer, the perception is unattractive.

Having eliminated the buyer, the lender and the seller, we're running out of people to pay a buyer agent. It's possible the buyer broker works without a fee, sort of pro bono, but a more likely scenario has his or her fee paid by the seller's broker.

The seller's broker?

It would be wonderful if purchasers paid buyer brokers directly, but that is not the marketplace reality. In the overwhelming majority of cases, buyer brokers are paid from funds set aside by seller agents. Here's how it works.

When broker Kirby listed the Campbell house for $150,000, Campbell agreed to pay a 6-percent commission if the property sold. The 6-percent figure was intended to be the entire brokerage fee, so if Kirby sold the property he would receive $9,000. If Kirby needs help selling the property, if a subagent brings in a buyer, then Kirby must pay part of his commission to the subagent.

If a buyer broker, we'll call him Burns, comes in with a client who wants the property, someone must pay his fee. The buyer lacks cash, lenders won't underwrite such expenses, and the seller is not obligated to pay more than a 6-percent commission. We're left with broker Kirby.

Kirby, being sane, would like to keep the entire 6-percent commission, but there won't be any commission if the property doesn't sell. Since he would have paid a cooperative fee to a subagent anyway, Kirby turns around and asks the seller if he can take a portion of the listing commission to pay the buyer's agent.

The seller wants to unload the property and since there is no additional marketing cost, he readily agrees.

At closing the buyer pays seller Campbell $150,000 for his home. Campbell pays a $9,000 marketing fee to broker Kirby. Kirby turns around and pays $4,500 to buyer broker Burns. Or it could be worked this way: Campbell pays $4,500 to broker Kirby and gives the buyers a $4,500 credit at closing.

So now we have concocted an arrangement where a home has been sold, both buyer and seller had separate representation, there were no excess seller concessions or brokerage fees, and all brokers were paid. Everyone should be happy, but all deals are not so simple.

PRACTICAL PROBLEMS

In the Campbell deal there was only one purchaser, but what if there were two people interested in the property? Suppose two bidders each offer $150,000, but one is located by a subagent while the other is represented by a buyer broker.

Seller Campbell now has two offers to consider. There is no difference in price, and we'll say that both buyers are equally well qualified. Which should he take?

If Campbell is logical, he'll take the deal from the subagent. After all, why should Campbell underwrite the cost of a buyer's agent, someone hired (financially speaking) to beat up the seller? For Campbell, the far better choice is to go with the subagent and work with a purchaser who is not separately represented.

Whether there is one buyer or two, we know that broker Kirby has offered to split the commission with a subagent. In a typical situation, this means that Kirby has stated up front just how much a subagent can make by participating in the deal.

Instead of offering "50 percent of the commission," Kirby is more likely to describe the subagent's fee in terms of the total sale ("Hey subagents. Bring in a buyer and earn 3 percent.") or as a dollar amount ("Subagents, if you help me sell the Campbell place I'll pay $4,500").

By describing the amount he is willing to pay subagents, Kirby has not disclosed the full size of his fee. He may be offering 50 percent of the total commission, or he may not.

When a buyer broker is involved in a transaction, he or she has no right to know the size of Kirby's fee. That's a private, contractual matter between Kirby and seller Campbell.

Because Kirby's fee is secret, buyer brokers may be in for a surprise if they demand half the commission. Imagine this scene at closing.

"And Mr. Kirby," says the closing agent, "Here is a check for the full amount due to you under your listing agreement with Mr. Campbell. The sale agreement to which you have consented requires that you pay half that amount to buyer broker Burns, so do you want to write him a check or just give him change?"

"Change!" bellows Burns. "What change? I want half the commission, the full commission, every penny."

"But Mr. Burns," says the closing agent. "Mr. Campbell and Mr. Kirby are good friends. They went to college together, belong to the same clubs, take two-couple vacations. Mr. Kirby has only charged $1 for his services. You are entitled to just 50 cents. Would you like that in the form of a check or coins? If you ask for coins, we'll need a receipt."

Absent a listing requirement to the contrary, buyer broker Burns not only lacks an automatic right to 50 percent of whatever Kirby is being paid, he has no right to *anything* Kirby receives.

If an offer is received that requires Kirby to pay out a portion of his commission to a buyer's agent, he can turn around and say to the seller, "Look, we have a deal. You agreed to pay me 6 percent if I found a buyer who was ready, willing and able to purchase the property under specific terms and conditions. There is no requirement in the listing agreement that I split my fee with a plumber, eye doctor, or buyer's representative. If you want this deal, pay the buyer broker from your funds, but don't touch my money."

Alternatively, Kirby might say to the seller, "I am obligated to take every possible step as your agent to market this property. I am not obligated to accept a violation of our listing contract and I do not wish to have it revised or modified. I will pay the buyer broker under protest so you can go to settlement, but then I'll sue to recover the money I pay to the buyer's agent."

Other interesting situations occur when the listing broker and a buyer broker bring in identical offers.

The deals are the same *to the owner* in terms of price and conditions, but they are different to broker Kirby. If Kirby's deal is selected, he pockets the full commission. If the owner wants the offer brought in by the buyer broker, then someone has to pay the buyer broker. If the homeowner says to Kirby, "Please split your fee," Kirby can say "But I've brought you an identical offer and I have no obligation to split the fee. If you want the buyer broker's deal, then you, the purchaser or both of you will have to pay that cost."

Another possible area of contention is the matter of splitting fees. The size of the selling agent's commission is not an issue because it was established when the property was listed. The buyer brokerage fee is also not a problem as long as the purchaser is willing to pay it in full.

What is an issue is when the seller or the seller's agent is effectively asked to underwrite a buyer brokerage commission. While the seller and the seller's agent have a contract between them, they have no agreement with the buyer or the buyer's agent.

Suppose Linhart makes an offer for the Patton home and within the offer is a requirement to split the listing commission 50/50 with a buyer broker. If Patton accepts the offer, all is well. But Patton and other sellers are simply not obligated to accept such an arrangement, any more than they are required to pay closing costs or points for the buyer. Patton has the right to make a counter-offer, perhaps one with a different commission split for the buyer's agent.

A question that continually arises with buyer representation is the myth of two fees. On the surface, if the seller pays a fee and the buyer pays a fee, then brokers are receiving two fees. So is it true that marketing expenses double when a buyer representative is involved in a transaction? Not at all.

The real issue is not how many fees are paid, but how the total amount compares with the fees that a traditional broker might charge. What difference does it make if a traditional broker charges $9,000 for a particular property, or if a traditional broker and a buyer agent together charge a total of $9,000?

CONFLICTS

Perhaps the most difficult issue within a buyer brokerage agreement concerns a highly unlikely issue: conflicts.

Suppose a purchaser likes only one house and that house is listed for sale with the purchaser's buyer broker. One solution would be for the broker to act as a disclosed dual agent and to represent both sides of the transaction. But if neither buyer nor seller are happy with this arrangement, then what? How does the broker handle such conflicts?

The best solution is for buyer brokers to disclose all current listings when a purchaser seeks representation. If any listed property looks even remotely desirable to the purchaser, then both the broker and the purchaser should examine the property and decide if any serious interest exists before a buyer agency agreement is reached.

If the buyer is not interested in any current listings, one problem is resolved. However, what if two months after a buyer agency contract goes into effect the broker lists a property for sale in which the purchaser is interested? Is the property off-limits to buyer clients? If a property is off-limits to purchasers, then aren't seller interests hurt?

Although brokers rarely find themselves in a situation where client buyers want to purchase properties from client sellers, at least in theory it can happen. One approach to resolving such an unlikely problem could be written into a buyer brokerage agreement, an arrangement that would work like this:

- If a buyer wants to purchase property listed by the broker, then the buyer brokerage agreement shall be null and void with regard to that particular property.
- If a buyer makes an offer on a home listed by the broker, the offer must include a copy of the entire buyer brokerage agreement so the seller is fully aware of the relationship between the buyer and the broker.
- If the deal goes to closing, any buyer agency fees paid to the broker shall be refunded to the purchaser.
- The purchaser must agree that the broker cannot be held liable for disclosing confidential information to the seller. Clearly the broker must disclose such information to the seller, and when it is disclosed, the buyer's interests are likely to be hurt.

While conflicts between buyer clients and seller clients are unlikely, other types of disputes may arise. Rather than turn to litigation, it is often much easier if binding arbitration is required in the buyer brokerage agreement. Such provisions can eliminate the time and hassles associated with the court system, especially if awards are limited to actual damages and payments for legal fees are prohibited.

Once an agreement is reached it is then the broker's job to find the right property, negotiate on the buyer's behalf, and work to get the best possible price and terms for the purchaser.

Unlike the listing broker or a subagent, the buyer broker is not tied to the seller's listing agreement. If the property lists for $215,000 and the buyer broker thinks it's worth $185,000, he can tell his client to offer less money. A seller's agent who made such a suggestion would clearly breach his agency obligations.

DISCOUNT BUYER BROKERAGE

In the late 1970s a small brokerage firm in northern Virginia won the right to rebate commissions to purchasers, a right that may have created a new form of representation: discount buyer brokerage.

Imagine that a $150,000 home is available with a 6-percent commission and Willman, a buyer broker, submits an offer for purchaser Jensen. The offer provides that Willman will receive a commission equal to 3 percent of the sale price ($4,500) and that from his commission Willman will pay 1.5 percent ($2,250) to buyer Jensen at settlement.

From the seller's perspective, Willman's offer to lower his commission makes the property more valuable but does not reduce the sale price. The listing broker's fee is unchanged.

State regulations generally prohibit payments or rebates by brokers to non-licensees. However, given that fees with clients are negotiable, why should sellers have the right to bargain over commissions, but not purchasers? Surely sellers can't object. The buyer agent is taking money out of his pocket to make the home more salable.

Buyer broker rebates are not a settled matter at this time, but invariably the issue will come up. If discounts called "rebates" are not allowed, then some brokers will take an approach that produces similar results without using the dreaded "r" word.

Suppose Simpson uses a buyer broker who charges $3,000 for his services. Suppose further that when the buyer agent submits an offer it includes a requirement for the seller to provide a $4,500 credit at closing. If the seller accepts the deal, then buyer Simpson has $4,500 for closing expenses, owes $3,000 to the broker, and has $1,500 remaining in his pocket. It may not be a rebate, but the economic result is identical.

THE LACK OF DEMAND

We have seen how buyer brokerage arrangements can work, and also how the concept can complicate a transaction. But if we are to look at the prime reason buyer brokers are not commonly used by purchasers, we have to look at performance.

Purchasers will hire buyer brokers when they can see that buyer representation makes a difference, one that can be measured in terms of bottom-line savings.

Separate representation sounds good, and it surely is attractive, but if the best a buyer broker can do is match deals that are otherwise available in the marketplace, then a buyer broker is unnecessary. To attract clients buyer brokers must offer more than the intellectual joy of separate representation. They must deliver lower prices and better terms.

When markets are hot and prices are rising, sellers have no shortage of offers, so why should they consider a low-ball deal with tough terms from a buyer broker? Seen from a buyer's perspective, if the market favors sellers, what advantages can buyer brokers offer?

When markets are slow and deals abound, who needs a buyer broker? Anyone with enough sophistication to hire a buyer representative will surely have sufficient savvy to carve out a good deal anyway. Rather than pay a buyer broker to find a property, why not call a seller agent? If a property is found, then an attorney or buyer broker can be hired on an hourly basis to help with negotiations.

The catch, of course, is that individuals who are sufficiently sophisticated to see the value of a buyer broker are also among those who are most likely to have the skills that will allow them to take advantage of a weak market. Conversely, less sophisticated purchasers who would profit most from the services of a buyer's agent are also the least likely to hire buyer brokers or to fully understand their benefits.

For buyers, the attraction of using *seller* representatives is that there is no *direct* cost to a purchaser. If one seller agent locates the right house, fine. But if a particular seller representative is not working well, buyers can find another seller representative without cost or obligation.

The point is not that residential buyer brokerage is unworkable, or that it is not worthwhile in selected cases; rather, the concept of buyer agency has not caused large numbers of purchasers to look up and say, "I want that service. It's important to me and I'm prepared to pay for it."

FUTURE TRENDS

As long as purchasers are in the marketplace there will always be buyer representation. The commercial real estate market has shown that such representation is valuable, but residential purchasers have yet to support the concept.

Looking ahead, it seems likely that buyer representation will spawn several trends:

First, listing agreements—to protect the public interest—will increasingly build in provisions so that buyer brokers can receive that portion of the commission usually set aside for subagents. In a buyer agency situation, for example, a seller might receive a credit equal to the co-op fee. The seller can provide a credit to the buyer at closing and the purchaser can then pay the buyer agent.

Second, to eliminate the onus of being paid a commission that is related to a co-op fee, some buyer brokers will instead arrange separate payment by purchasers. Since buyers normally lack such funds, offers through buyer agents will include a provision requiring the seller to pay a portion of the purchaser's closing costs. Those closing costs—whatever it is that the buyer must pay at settlement—can include buyer brokerage fees. The attraction of this scenario is that the seller pays his broker and the buyer separately pays his representative.

Third, buyer brokerage will be most successful in large markets (where there are enough clients to support buyer brokerage firms) and among well-to-do, sophisticated buyers who are used to working with consultants and paying for professional services.

Fourth, faced with a deal that includes a provision to pay buyer closing expenses, selling brokers may *elect* to reduce commissions when buyer brokers are involved in a transaction. The reasoning works like this: The seller must pay the buyer's closing costs to make the transaction work, otherwise the purchaser will not have enough money to pay a buyer brokerage fee. In effect, the selling broker wants the deal made, and whether a portion of the commission goes to a cooperating broker or a buyer broker, at least there is a deal. If the seller's agent does not reduce his commission, then there might be too many costs in the transaction to make the sale attractive to the homeowner.

Fifth, the use of state-mandated disclosure forms declaring that a broker represents a seller or buyer will be used throughout the country. The use of disclosure forms, at first opposed by much of the brokerage community, is now recognized as a major weapon against lawsuits and legal actions.

Sixth, residual efforts to ban buyer brokers from MLS systems will disappear. Such efforts restrain trade and open the real estate community to legal action.

Seventh, buyer brokerage will remain what it has always been in the residential field, a pleasant curiosity with great potential and little general impact—unless the rules change.

WHAT IF THE RULES CHANGE?

Buyer representation is not a significant factor in most areas today, and as long as agency/subagency relationships are both common and accepted there is little reason to believe that buyer agency will become widespread. But what would happen if the real estate industry decided that after years of working with agency and subagency, maybe it would be better to revert to separate representation for buyers and sellers?

California has one of the most unusual disclosure laws in the country, one that allows brokers to identify themselves as seller agents, buyer agents, or dual agents. In addition, many MLS networks in the state do not require a unilateral offer of subagency to list properties.

What is an MLS without subagency? It can be considered a database showing what properties have sold in the past and what properties are available today.

And if agents and subagents don't use an MLS, then who does? Brokers who represent sellers and others who represent buyers brokers.

The California experience provides a growing body of evidence that subagency is not required to make an MLS work or to produce industry profits. In addition, events in California disprove several theories.

No one wants buyer representation. Given sufficient education and adequate disclosure forms, a demand for buyer agency has been demonstrated.

Without subagency, MLS systems will be less valuable selling tools for brokers. California MLS networks are restricted to brokers, so brokers still have an exclusive marketing tool that self-sellers and non-brokers can't use. Since all California brokers may join a local MLS—whether or not they belong to a particular real estate group—MLS membership does not offer a competitive advantage to any individual broker, whether they represent sellers or buyers.

Buyer agency hurts large firms. Large companies in California, and small ones, are still in business.

To succeed, an MLS must have a pro-seller orientation. California MLS networks no longer have a pro-seller slant and they still function successfully.

California has been a trend-setter in many areas and if agency-free MLS networks are successful, then the concept will spread. Given client-neutral MLS networks, fuller disclosure statements, and increased public experience with separate representation, buyer brokerage can become more acceptable. Whether it will also become more desirable is something only the marketplace can determine.

10

For Sale By Owner

Few activities represent a greater threat to the real estate community than real estate sales by owners without broker participation. Deals by self-sellers discomfort the industry because it is hard evidence that every deal does not require a broker.

A 1987 study by the National Association of Realtors shows that FISBO (for sale by owner) transactions account for 20 percent of all residential sales. Most self-sellers, said the study, are in it for the money, specifically the money homeowners don't want to spend for brokerage services.

A study published in *Consumer Reports* (July 1990) showed that of 72,000 readers polled, 18 percent sold homes without a broker.

In an environment with a surplus of brokers and agents hotly competing for a limited number of transactions, FISBOs make the market smaller. To give an idea of how much smaller, suppose that 3.5 million existing homes are sold each year. If 20 percent are FISBO deals, then 700,000 homeowners are selling properties without a broker *each year!* If the average home sells for $100,000 and a typical commission equals 6 percent of the selling price, then the FISBO market represents $4.2 billion in lost brokerage revenues—more than $80 million per week.

But even lost dollars do not explain the angst caused by FISBO deals. Worse than the money involved is the precedent such transactions document and the discomforting questions they raise.

People hire brokers because they believe that brokers offer a service homeowners cannot perform, do not want to perform, or do not perform as well. FISBOs demonstrate that the services of a broker can be duplicated by individuals outside the real estate community and that if the standard by which we measure marketplace success is the sale of a property, then some homesellers can pass this test without assistance from brokers and agents.

Conversely, while 20 percent of all deals may involve self-sellers, FISBOs actually have a larger impact than sale figures suggest for the following reasons:

First, 20 percent of all sales involve FISBOs but not every FISBO succeeds. If we combine successful FISBOs with would-be FISBOs, then more than 20 percent of all homeowners start out selling by themselves.

Second, not all FISBO deals are brokerless. Many self-described FISBOs actually receive help from brokers in the form of signs, contract forms, negotiating help and advertising.

A careful look at the FISBO movement suggests the existence of at least five sub-groups, each with a different purpose, interest and marketplace importance:

- Owners who sell successfully by themselves.
- Those who successfully market their property but wish they hired a broker.
- Self-sellers who are unable to market their properties.
- Owners who use FISBO status to get better deals from brokers.
- Assisted sales where owners and brokers work jointly to market properties.

THE BROKER'S NIGHTMARE

He may look just like everyone else, but in the eyes of the real estate community Mr. King is an ogre of the first rank. It is not that he has claws, gives off radiation, or commits heinous crimes, but rather that he is an astute self-seller in a local marketplace where informed FISBOs have leverage and power.

For nearly a decade King lived in the Crestmont subdivision, a group of 1,000 townhouses built in 1982. When it came time to sell, King knew that his property—like other three bedroom, two-bath end-units in Crestmont—would sell for about $148,000.

To get the largest possible profit King must charge a top price and cut costs. Of all the expenses he faces, none is bigger than the 7-percent fee charged by local brokers, a $10,360 cost if King sells his home for $148,000. Rather than hire a broker, King decides to sell by himself.

Pricing. Units such as King's have been selling for $148,000 so King decides to ask $151,000. If a buyer offers less, at least King has room to negotiate.

Who Shouldn't Be a FISBO

Not every seller should be a FISBO, just as not everyone should do their own taxes. In particular, the following types of sellers should avoid FISBO marketing.

Passive Sellers: Marketing real estate is an activity that requires salesmanship and negotiating skills. If you don't like to bargain and haggle, hire a broker.

Down Sellers: Self-selling seems most common when markets are stable or declining, which is precisely the time when homes are hardest to sell and brokerage services are most valuable. If the local market is quiet you'll need all the help you can get.

Long-Distance Sellers: Remote self-selling is one of the worst possible ideas in real estate. If you're not there, who can answer questions, show the property, or bargain?

The Upper Crust: As homes become more expensive they tend to take longer to sell, so if time is valuable it may actually be cheaper to have a broker market your property rather than invest endless hours doing it yourself.

Personality Plus: Selling real estate is a business process. If the central motivation for being a self-seller is ego, then it becomes easy to satisfy the soul by making whatever deal comes along, perhaps including one that isn't so good.

Condition. To get the best possible price, King paints the front door and several rooms. He also orders a special trash pick-up to get rid of old furniture and accumulated boxes.

Marketing. King creates printed hand-outs that closely resemble those used by area brokers and invests $150 in professionally-made signs, one for the front yard and several "arrow" signs showing how to get to his house. He also advertises, a $60 expense for each Sunday insertion.

Contracts. King doesn't have a broker, so he hires a local real estate attorney to provide a local contract form and to explain what it means. For help with the transaction, King expects to pay $450 in legal fees based on an hourly cost of $150.

Financing. A major benefit offered by brokers is that they are familiar with loan rates and terms. King isn't, so he calls various lenders and gets the names of local loan officers. Considering the property's price and current interest rates, the lenders estimated how much a prospective buyer will need in terms of income and cash. Several even prepare flyers for King showing different ways the property can be financed.

It takes several open houses, many phone calls, and a few weeks, but King eventually finds his buyer. With the help of his attorney, Mr. McMillan, King has both a deal and considerable savings. He cut his marketing costs by more than $10,000, but he did not sell his home without costs. He had to pay for signs, advertising, legal advice and other costs, and he also had to invest his time and energy.

King is a unique self-seller because he prepared both his property and himself to get the best possible deal. He had good fortune in the marketplace, but he also worked hard to create his success.

THE SAVINGS ILLUSION

For McMillan, King's attorney, self-selling seemed like a good idea. With a property worth $300,000, McMillan determined that he could save $21,000 by avoiding a 7-percent commission.

Who Gets the Commission?

Surely one reason for selling homes as a FISBO is to pocket the broker's commission. Homes have a market value and whether sold by owners or brokers, the market value—at least in theory—should not change.

In real life, the person who gets the commission is likely to be determined by the local market. In a seller's market, where demand is strong and prices are rising, owners keep the brokerage commission. In a mixed market, that is, one with ongoing sales and moderate price increases, the fee is up for grabs. Whoever negotiates best gets the commission. If the seller is strong then the fee will be reflected in a higher price. If the buyer bargains well, then the house sells at a discount. If buyer and seller are equally matched, then the fee's value is likely to be split.

If the marketplace features poor sales and stagnant or declining prices, then the purchaser will pocket the fee in the form of a large discount.

It took McMillan four months to sell his house, but he thought at least he had the satisfaction of saving a big commission. Or did he?

When McMillan calculated his costs, he found some disturbing news. With all the energy spent showing the house and handling phone calls, if time is money, then selling a home without a broker can sometimes be expensive.

If McMillan spent 12 hours per week dealing with lenders, brokers and would-be purchasers, then at $150 per hour—his usual billing rate—he lost the opportunity to earn $1,800 a week, or $7,200 per month. Over a period of four months he was out $28,800—far more than any broker would have charged for a full package of marketing services.

McMillan also determined that in addition to his time, there were costs for advertising ($180 per month) and signs ($150). In total, over four months McMillan's costs were roughly $29,670: $28,800 for lost income, $720 for advertising ($180 × 4) and $150 for signs.

A few weeks after his home went to closing, a client told McMillan that he wanted to sell by himself. "I'm not sure," McMillan counseled his client, "I sold by myself, got my price, but if I had to do it again, I think I'd opt for the best broker I could find.

"I type faster than my secretary," he continued, "but I make more money as a lawyer. In the same fashion, if your time is valuable, carefully consider self-selling. It can work, but it may be less than a bargain."

THE IRRATIONAL FISBO

Some self-sellers are both FISBOs and FAILBOs—FISBOs because they are trying to market a home without a broker, and FAILBOs because they botch the job.

Consider Wilburn, a homeowner with an eye for the bottom line and a foul understanding of the marketing system. If you were to speak with Wilburn, you would quickly understand that his property is for sale on his terms, $150,000, an amount which goes entirely to the seller. There is nothing in that price for brokerage fees, closing costs, loan expenses, or taxes. Wilburn is a FAILBO because, in addition to having a strange view of real estate pricing, his selling skills and perceptions are completely distorted, as illustrated by the following dialogue.

Question: Mr. Wilburn, you are asking $150,000 for your home when like properties are selling for $140,000?

Wilburn. So what? I need $40,000 in cash to buy my next property and that means I have to sell for $150,000. Besides, if the Clarks can sell for $190,000 over in Berkley, I should get $150,000.

Question. But you don't live in Berkley.

Wilburn. What's your point? This house is just as big as that thing the Clarks sold and it has a better view of the rendering plant.

Question. If you want a top price, why don't you at least paint and fix up your home?

Wilburn. If I paint now whoever buys this place will just cover up what I've done with new colors or wallpaper. Cleaning out the basement, trimming hedges, getting rid of that dead tree, and stopping that drip under the kitchen sink are needless tasks. People should just imagine what the place will look like after they buy it.

Question. If you want to impress prospective buyers, why not put up professionally-made "for sale" signs and advertise like brokers?

Wilburn. First of all, the hardware store sells perfectly good cardboard signs. As for advertising, that's just a waste of money. People who want to live in this neighborhood come by all the time.

Question. Will you get an attorney to help with the contract?

Wilburn. Your willingness to spend my money is simply unlimited. The very same hardware store that carries signs also stocks sale contracts.

Question. Suppose I offered $140,000 for your place, would you take it?

Wilburn. I'd rather be frozen up to my hairline in spit.

Question. Undoubtedly that is a thought shared by many who have known you. Let's try this. If I offer $150,000 will you pay the transfer taxes and two points?

Wilburn. I keep hearing this expression, "You pay, you pay." I'm the seller, it's my job to collect. It's your job to pay. Let's not confuse our roles.

Question. If a broker brought in a purchaser, would you at least pay a small commission, something less than brokers usually get?

Wilburn. I'm not in the "you pay" mode. If a broker wants to do a favor for a friend, that's great. But don't expect me to pay for a service I don't need. This place will sell. Ask yourself my friend: How many former mortuaries with three bedrooms and a wonderful parlor are available these days?

Although Wilburn doesn't know it, his home is unattractive, poorly located, and grossly overpriced. Then too, if someone stumbles across the property and actually wants to buy it, they must deal with Mr. Wilburn, a man whose photo can be found in the dictionary illustrating the term "irrational."

FISBO LEVERAGE

Somewhere between King the prepared, McMillan the dissatisfied, and Wilburn the crotchety, there are FISBOs who know the meaning of leverage. These are homeowners who would rather not be self-sellers, but who use FISBO status to gain marketplace strength.

When Emerson asked about selling his home he found that local brokers were united on price. Everyone said the same thing—6 percent. No bargaining, no discounts and no substitutes.

Rankled by such uniformity, Emerson decided to become a self-seller. He bought signs, made flyers, and advertised in the local papers. As soon as the signs went up, the curious began to call and among those callers were several brokers.

Emerson was not an agent but he could effectively co-op. As brokers called or visited to seek a listing, Emerson made this offer: You can show the property with an open listing and if I close with your buyer, then I'll pay a 3 percent brokerage fee.

Some brokers objected, but Emerson pointed out that if the property had been listed with another broker, they would typically receive a 3-percent co-op fee anyway. Whether the co-op fee came from a broker or an owner, Emerson argued, the money is still spendable. Emerson wouldn't sign anything but an open listing, so he won the argument.

Emerson was prepared to sell by himself, but when a broker sought a co-op deal with an open listing, Emerson agreed. His goal was to sell the property, cut costs, and increase his profit, something he could accomplish with a co-op deal and the appearance of FISBO status.

ASSISTED SALES

Not every FISBO has a "we-versus-them" attitude. Certain homesellers prefer to work with brokers but on something less than a full-service basis. Whether such individuals are truly FISBOs is a matter open to debate, but the important point is that assisted sales represent a halfway point between full broker representation and unqualified FISBO status.

For homeowner Hemphill there were three choices when it came time to sell: do it himself, sell through a broker, or sell *with* a broker.

Hemphill felt no one could show a home better than an owner and he also believed that he had three classic marketplace advantages: his home was well located, well maintained, and well priced. In other words, an easy sale.

That said, Hemphill was not one to bargain and he was entirely unfamiliar with the mechanics of homeselling. After speaking to various brokers, Hemphill elected to use a flat fee broker who would advertise and handle negotiations. Hemphill would show the property.

For Hemphill the deal worked because his property was attractive, he was skillful and gracious when showing the house, and he had the support he needed from a broker. He paid a brokerage fee, but he paid far less than a traditional broker might have charged.

THE FISBO OPPORTUNITY

There is no doubt that FISBO sales represent a significant part of today's real estate marketplace, but whether the FISBO movement will grow is open to question.

A study by lenders in Maine during the 1970s showed that FISBOs represented 20 percent of the market. A 1978 survey of for-sale classified ads in Montgomery County, Maryland, just outside Washington, DC, found that 16.2 percent of all notices were placed by FISBOs.

These figures—plus the more recent NAR and Consumer Reports studies—suggest that FISBOs have always been part of the marketplace and that FISBOs will be with us in the future. That said, self-selling is likely to face two contradictory trends in the 1990s.

One tendency is the move toward complexity. Fifteen, ten, and even five years ago, selling real estate was a relatively simple process. That just isn't the situation any more. Real estate agreements have gotten longer and longer, reflecting such matters as zoning, environmental concerns, buyer representation, open housing, misrepresentation, deposit interest, and local regulations. Selling property today without professional assistance from a broker or lawyer is like trying to cut doctor bills by removing your own kidney.

A second trend that will influence FISBO sales is the movement away from a monolithic brokerage community.

It was not so long ago that every broker in town offered the same services at the same prices. That, too, has changed. Now brokerage competition resembles the auto industry, with many makes, models and prices from which to choose.

The 1987 NAR survey shows that self-sellers and those who use brokers are virtually alike in terms of age, income and previous homeownership experience. If homesellers are so much alike, why then do some choose to be FISBOs? The most common reason is money. Many simply have no desire to pay a commission or fee.

The alternatives are fairly clear when the choice is only between self-selling and the use of a full-service broker. But if the alternative is self-selling versus the use of a discount broker, flat-fee broker, or a traditional broker who cuts his price, then the decision-making process becomes less certain.

If the proportion of FISBO transactions grows in the 1990s then traditional brokers will lose business. A more likely scenario is that FISBO sales will continue to represent 20 percent of the marketplace, but that FISBOs will increasingly use some brokerage services. The net effect will be to increase the demand for flat-fee brokers, discount brokers, and traditional brokers who act as consultants.

11

Challenging the MLS

In the office where these words are written is something called a Brunsviga Midget, a 1910 black and silver machine that looks like a horizontal meat grinder. To make it work you push some spokes, turn a crank and ultimately the machine will add, subtract, multiply and divide.

The Brunsviga sits on a shelf replaced by a pocket calculator while nearby a 1917 Corona portable typewriter that folds in half has been dumped in favor of a computer. Unlike the Corona, the computer doesn't fold, but then you don't need the arms of a blacksmith to make it work.

The old machines are beautifully finished, cleverly engineered, made in the USA, and emblematic of a different era. Today our national emphasis has shifted from manufacturing to services, and bulky machines have been replaced with high-tech electronics.

In the real estate industry, MLS networks have gone high-tech. Instead of listing cards and bulky books, most MLS networks are now on-line databases. If you need to find three-bedroom colonials priced at $160,000 or less, the computer can pick out every listing in the system within seconds.

Combine listings with pictures, something that already has begun to happen, and photo tours can replace the old and unproductive process of driving a buyer to 50 homes. Why waste gas, time and shoe leather when buyers can sit in a broker's office, look at hundreds of houses arranged by price, location or any other factor, and pick the five or ten that seem most appealing?

In the not-so-distant future, brokers will be able to use a single computer not only to connect with the local MLS, but also to combine buyer records from a credit bureau with financial qualification standards from many lenders. Mesh such information together and it will be possible to calculate the borrower's buying power—all within the time it takes to make coffee.

Press a few more buttons and a standardized contract complete with names and addresses can be printed out immediately. If a buyer wants to change some wording or add a few clauses, no problem. In many states—but not all—brokers will be able to directly customize contracts to meet the buyer's instructions.

The computer revolution that will make MLS networks more valuable suffers only from one flaw: computer programs can also be used by people outside the real estate industry, a fact that may produce new forms of competition.

COMMUNITY HOUSING NETWORKS

A central value of MLS systems is that they provide not only information, they provide information exclusively to member brokers. But what would happen if a corporation, union or civic association decided to track home sales? Such information is entirely public in most states and can be easily entered on the increasingly cheaper and faster computers introduced each year.

From the corporate perspective, rising home prices make it difficult to attract individuals who want both a job and a home. Another corporate concern, relocations, is a costly matter where companies often spend $30,000 or more to move a single employee. In fact, housing costs are so significant that some companies have actually established real estate subsidiaries to collect referral fees when employees move.

Unions, too, have a natural interest in housing costs if only because such expenses are likely to be the largest monthly bill faced by individual members.

Unlike in the past, organized labor can no longer provide assured job security, top wages, or increased benefits. It's tough to bargain for more benefits when the steel industry is contracting, to argue that unionization is necessary when non-union auto plants are thriving, or to seek higher wages when local tax initiatives limit pay increases for state and local workers. As a result, union membership is in decline around the country. In 1945 union members represented 35 percent of the workforce. By 1987, only 17 percent of the workforce were union members. Between 1980 and 1987 alone, union rolls were cut by 4 million people.

Unions are now faced with a basic question: if they can't provide traditional values such as job security and better wages, who needs them? Viewed another way, what can unions provide to members that workers cannot get directly from companies or government? Specialized services, including real estate services made practical by computerization, may be one answer.

Rather then depend solely on the real estate community for marketing services, corporations, unions or even individuals could develop an alternative, what might be called a "community housing network." Such a system could not only make property information widely available, it could also be combined with training and education classes to create a one-stop consumer resource.

The first step is to create a basic database to start the system, something that can be done by checking local home sales for the past year or two.

The next step is to offer separate one-night real estate seminars for buyers and sellers. Such classes need not duplicate traditional real estate instruction because system users will not represent others, list homes, or take a state exam. Instead the classes can concentrate on direct consumer issues such as how to prepare a home for sale, how to get the best price, how to bargain, where to get financing, and how to use professionals such as lawyers, structural inspectors, and brokers.

The third step is to publicize the system to potential users. Considering that corporations and unions deal with large numbers of people, attracting attention is a relatively simple process.

As to fees, such a network can be run as a service without charge because typical business economics may not apply. Most sponsoring agencies will set up systems to provide a service rather than to make a profit. If fees are charged they are likely to be modest. Reasonable costs might include:

- $50 to list a home on the system for three months.
- $50 to attend a buyers' or sellers' educational seminar. Potential users will have to complete at least one class before using the system, a requirement designed to give buyers and sellers some equality in the marketplace.
- $10 per month to rent professionally-made "for sale" signs.
- $25 for buyers who want to access the system for a period of three months.

Once the system is in operation it will work much like a conventional MLS but with one difference: there is no exclusivity for brokers. Instead, sellers can list their homes directly, buyers can look for properties without necessarily going through a broker, and if a buyer and seller are interested in making a deal, then each can turn to such professional advisors as they require—perhaps an attorney or legal clinic paid hourly, a structural engineer selected by the purchaser, or a broker to act as a consultant to either side.

Within a community housing network, agency and sub-agency are options, not requirements for brokers. Brokers who list a property in a network can co-op with other brokers, but subagency is not automatic.

The economic effects of a community housing network could be profound. If owners have a reasonable, effective home marketing system, then brokers will not only have to compete against each other for listings, they will also have to compete with an alternative marketing concept. Such competition will undoubtedly exert a clear downward pressure on commission rates and enlarge the number of owners who elect to act as self-sellers. In effect, the number of dollars coming into the real estate community could fall.

In those cases where buyers and sellers deal directly with one another, there is no broker and therefore no brokerage fee.

Sellers will be able to offer their properties for sale at a lower price than comparable properties represented by brokers, but often with a better net result.

For example, if two similar townhouses are available in the same subdivision, and one is priced at $150,000 and the other is offered for $145,000, then the probability is that the lower-priced home will sell more quickly. Certainly buyers will be happier with a lower price and sellers may find that it is better to sell for a plain vanilla price of $145,000 rather than $150,000 less a brokerage commission of 6 percent ($9,000) or 7 percent ($10,500).

How realistic is a multiple listing service not run or organized by the brokerage community? The military, under the Joint Armed Forces Housing Referral Office (JAFRO), effectively runs such a service, which lists thousands of properties that can be bought, rented, sublet, or shared throughout the Washington, DC area. Additional JAFRO networks exist in other cities with several military facilities and large military populations.

Whether the real estate community should be particularly concerned about privately-run MLS programs is as yet unclear. The mere existence of a private MLS undoubtedly eliminates some sale and rental opportunities for brokers. At the same time, even with a sophisticated program like JAFRO, two points should be remembered:

First, brokers absolutely dominate the Washington-area real estate market despite the fact that many local residents qualify for JAFRO services.

Second, many brokers use JAFRO. Instead of viewing JAFRO as a competitive threat, brokers commonly enter their listings in both local MLS networks as well as the JAFRO system. JAFRO may not be run by the brokerage community, but it is a marketing tool, one that many brokers use effectively.

12

Mortgage Fees:
The Unwanted Burden

It might have happened this way: One day two mortgage lenders—we'll call them Green and Brown—were sitting around the office. With so much competition it was tough to get business and thinking about how to get more loans, an idea slowly emerged.

"Most of our business comes from brokers," said Green. "So why don't we evoke self-interest and just pay these guys each time they send in a borrower."

"You can't do that," said Brown. "The government says we can't pay a fee for referrals. Sometimes I wonder, though, if there isn't a way around the rules, something legal but something that would bring in business and give us an edge over other lenders."

The two hashed out various plans and schemes, refined ideas, and tested notions back and forth, until finally Green came up with an idea.

"Look, if we can't pay brokers for referrals, maybe someone else could simply pay them a fee for service. What about buyers? They're hit with so many fees and charges that they won't even notice one more. Besides, if a buyer voluntarily pays money to a broker for services, no referral fee is involved."

"That's great," said Brown. "You've just concocted a scheme to generate more money for real estate brokers. How about more money for lenders?"

"Here's how we get our slice of the action and eliminate other lenders at the same time," Green replied. "We make it easier for brokers to charge a fee. We stock them with information on loan programs, rates and terms. We update everything by computer so we don't have to waste so much time visiting broker offices. We can even supply computer programs so brokers can plug in some numbers and see how much prospects can borrow.

"And this is the good part," Green continued. "We can make money. We charge brokers for the information and programs we offer, something modest so brokers buy into the system. And then, of course, we get lots of loans.

"Think about it. A buyer comes into the broker's office. The buyer has seen a house, wants to make a deal, and now we come to the slight matter of money. Where can the buyer get those dollars?

"And right there, sitting in the broker's office, is the magic money machine. Press a few buttons and out pops today's rates and terms. Plug in the buyer's income and debts, and within a few moments our little electronic box estimates how much the buyer can borrow.

"Now if you were the buyer, and you just knew that right there was a piece of paper from a genuine, never fail, always correct computer estimating your borrowing strength and showing that you could buy the house of your dreams—wouldn't you take that loan?

"And if you were a broker, a broker who eats regularly only when houses sell, would you stop that buyer and say, 'wait, don't sign, there may be a better loan down the street.'"

Brown thought about his friend's ideas for a few minutes and then asked, "Are you saying we would make a loan commitment based on the numbers put into the computer by a broker?"

"We'll make a conditional commitment. If the borrower's income figures are wrong, if there are credit problems, or if the property doesn't appraise, well then we just won't go through with the deal."

"But one question," said Brown. "You said the brokers could make money. How?"

"The broker can charge prospects for using the service."

"But brokers never charge for mortgage information," said Brown. "What makes you think they'll start now."

"You're missing the point. We're giving them a pretext to charge buyers, but it's not our business whether or not brokers charge fees. All we care about is beating out other lenders and getting the highest possible rates and fees. We're not running a charity for brokers.

"Think about it this way. We don't care if brokers charge for loan information, but you can bet that organized brokerage groups will defend to the death their right to charge such fees. If they don't defend fees for mortgages, then maybe someone will get the idea that brokers should be prohibited from selling insurance or the other services they offer.

"I'm telling you, we'll look like heroes to every agent in town."

"I like it," said Brown. "We cut out other lenders, we make no absolute commitments, referral fees are not an issue because we're not paying anyone for anything, we have few worries about someone else's rates, we haven't violated any laws, and the best part is that we get to tell brokers that we're going to help them make a few dollars. How can we lose?"

LEGAL RIGHTS VERSUS MARKETPLACE REALITIES

The most basic truth in the mortgage business is that mortgage providers are dependent on brokers and agents for referrals. Cut such referrals and many lenders will need a different line of work.

Seen from a different perspective, if you were a mortgage lender you would want to attract as much broker attention as possible. Office visits, seminars, rate-change announcements, and ongoing coddling would all be part of your day.

Some lenders have gone further. To capture additional referrals and to edge out rivals, several already provide brokers with computer terminals. Press a button and you can find a variety of programs with a corresponding variety of rates and terms. Feed in the right information about income, assets, and debits and you can quickly see how much prospective buyers might borrow and, therefore, how much they can pay for property.

Brokers, seeking new ways to maximize revenues, have

looked at the time and facilities used to provide mortgage information and some have concluded that loan advice is a commodity for which lenders or consumers should pay. The Department of Housing and Urban Development (HUD), for its part, has issued three opinions that support such fees.

- HUD determined in 1984 that brokers can establish an in-house mortgage information program and charge lenders a fee to be included; in essence, a kind of rent for the use of brokerage facilities.
- In 1986, HUD provided an opinion saying that brokers can charge *borrowers* for mortgage loan information and services, providing such payments are voluntary.
- In 1990, HUD reaffirmed its earlier positions. Brokers, said HUD, can offer loans providing they disclose fees, that fees are voluntary, and that buyers are made aware that loans are available from sources other than the broker. Another idea from HUD, one which may be formalized as a regulation by 1992, requires brokers to open up their systems so that any interested lender could participate. If enacted, the rule would end single-lender systems.

Thus it's clear that brokers can charge a fee for the time and facilities they use to provide mortgage information and services. It's equally clear that the Real Estate Settlement and Procedures Act—"RESPA" to industry insiders—bans so-called "naked referrals," payments or receipts for merely sending a buyer to a given lender in exchange for a fee, kickback, thing of value or other consideration.

"In our mind," says Stephen D. Driesler, senior vice-president for government affairs with the National Association of Realtors, "a referral is sending somebody, a customer, without providing any service. A fee for that in the loan origination system is illegal. It is made illegal by RESPA. We have no problem with that position. In fact we very much support that position."

Driesler argues that when brokers provide additional services they should be entitled to extra compensation. He also says brokers who sell houses and find mortgage money for buyers are really performing two jobs.

"There is the job of finding a buyer for a piece of property. That deserves to be compensated. There is the job of finding funds for the buyer, a separate and distinct job that also deserves to be compensated. The issue boils down to: Is there anything inherently wrong with the same person or the same entity performing both of those jobs, being compensated for both of those jobs?"

Driesler contends that brokers can charge for loan information as long as two factors exist: complete disclosure and a total absence of "tying" arrangements that require the use of a particular product or service.

"As long as those two factors are present," Driesler says, "and the consumer wants these services and is willing to pay for traditional services, then we think it is completely acceptable and, in fact, we think there are a lot of advantages to the consumer in this arrangement."

Should a broker be paid for providing generic information, or only when a particular product or lender is selected?

"The broker or sales agent," says Driesler, "is generally familiar with the mortgage market. They have traditionally provided generic information."

"But when they go beyond that and start doing more sophisticated analysis, when they start actually taking loan applications, filling out the paper work, assisting the buyer in the actual selection of a loan product that suits their needs, working with the lender to originate a loan commitment, then that is additional service above and beyond what they ordinarily provide and should be compensated."

Within the brokerage community, fees for mortgage information and advice have received an enormous amount of attention. Brokers resolutely defend their right to charge for their time and facilities. Simultaneously, few brokers today actually charge for loan information or placements.

To explain this apparent conflict, the issue of fees for mortgage information and advice must be viewed from three perspectives: territory, conflicts, and claims.

TERRITORY

If there is a single quality that defines professions it is the zest for turf and territory. Medical doctors battle with chiropractors and podiatrists, psychologists argue with psychiatrists, optometrists fight with ophthalmologists, and paralegals feud with lawyers. In each case proponents of one side or another can explain in glowing detail why their position alone is righteous and how it protects the public interest. Left unstated is the not-so-slight matter of fees, payments, and professional income.

Brokers also have territory and like good professionals they make a point of defending their vested interests. In the case of mortgage information fees, signals from the brokerage community are decidedly mixed.

If the question is should brokers have the right to charge fees for loan advice and other services, the answer from the real estate community is yes. If the question is changed slightly, if brokers are asked whether they actually charge for loan information, the most common answer today is no.

Why the big contrast? Just look at the way brokers make their money.

Most people are paid bi-weekly, but such comfortable rituals are virtually unknown in real estate. Among brokers and agents, the equation is different: performance equals income. If you don't perform, you don't get paid.

This Darwinian formula may seem cruel yet it offers at least one comforting advantage: If you perform, if you can buy or sell, you can generate enormous fees.

The trouble with this system is that fee income is rarely steady. Sometimes the marketplace is strong, but when interest rates rise or local businesses close, then sales and income drop. As much as brokers may enjoy the prospect of unlimited income, they naturally prefer to hedge marketplace slides. To beat bankrupting dry spells many brokers not only help others buy and sell real estate, they offer other services as well.

One natural service is property management. Handling rental properties enables brokers to collect a fee when the property is first leased and each time a monthly rental check arrives. The dollars may not be as grand as sale commissions, but at least the money is steady and in an uncertain world regular income has value. In addition, management agreements commonly provide that if the property is sold during the lease term, the broker can collect a full brokerage fee.

Another way to stabilize earnings and generate additional dollars is to offer non-brokerage services. Insurance is often a

good choice because homeowner's coverage (fire, theft and liability insurance) is required when buyers finance real estate.
The buyer needs insurance, the broker has insurance available,
and seller interests are entirely undisturbed, so if a home buyer
elects to purchase insurance from a broker, everyone is happy.
If it happens that a home buyer also needs life insurance and
auto coverage, that's fine too.

For brokers, then, it is the *right* to charge for mortgage
information that is supremely important. Take away that right
and the possibility arises that other activities will also be prohibited, activities that have long assured economic stability for
many brokers.

CONFLICTS

Since real estate brokerage is an entrepreneurial activity it
seems logical to believe that brokers would welcome the opportunity to charge for loan information. In the vernacular of high
finance, charge for mortgage advice and information and you
can create a new and possibly lush "profit center."

Charging for mortgage information also may create something else: a variety of conflicts and liabilities that offset any
possible gains.

No one doubts that to be a competent broker or agent, an
individual must understand the lending process. A broker or
agent should *at least* know about FHA and VA loans, conventional financing, second trusts, and adjustable-rate mortgages
(ARMs).

Knowing about loans is not an idle requirement because
brokers are not hired to sell houses. In the typical case brokers
are hired to find a buyer "ready, willing and able" to purchase
property at a price and terms acceptable to the seller.

But how do you know if a prospect is "able" to buy? If Bookman sees a $300,000 house, likes it, and signs an offer to pur-
chase the property, we at least know he is ready and willing.
What if Bookman lacks savings, isn't in the wills of the rich or
famous, and only earns $14,000 a year? He may be ready and
willing, but he is surely unable to buy. To avoid the havoc
unqualified buyers can create, brokers routinely require a financial statement to support a purchase offer.

In a situation where a buyer cannot get financing, the goals of both sellers and brokers can be viewed as jointly thwarted. But tallying who won and who lost in a broken deal is not so easy when the buyer has made payments to a broker.

Suppose broker Fisher lists a $150,000 property owned by Parkington. Fisher is Parkington's agent and naturally wants to get the best possible deal for his client. Fisher works to sell Parkington's property and when buyer Nelson says he wants it, Fisher is more than happy to write up the papers.

Nelson cannot pay cash for the property, so he must find financing. At this point Fisher says, "We are part of the First Trumpet Underwriting Corporation. Over here we have the Decibel 6000 computer system. We just put your information into the machine and in a few minutes it will tell us how much you can borrow with the best rates and terms I have. It's just $50 to use, so let's see how much you can borrow before someone else makes an offer on the property."

Sufficiently entranced and wanting the house, Nelson writes out a $50 check and gives his information to broker Fisher. Fisher enters such data as Nelson's income, assets, debts, and cash deposits into the system. Moments later the machine determines that Nelson can borrow $130,000 with an adjustable-rate mortgage but only $126,000 with fixed-rate financing.

At this point broker Fisher is in an enviable position. He has a prospect who wants to buy plus he has a variety of confidential information that tells him how much Nelson can afford.

Seeing how much he can borrow, Nelson takes the maximum loan amount and combines it with his available cash to make an offer of $140,000 for Parkington's property. Fisher takes the offer to Parkington who questions if it's the best possible deal.

"Look," says Fisher, "your property has been for sale for several months, we have a buyer, and if this offer is not accepted we may not get another for some time. We ran this guy's numbers through the computer and we know that $130,000 is the most he can borrow from us. Combine his borrowing ability with his cash on hand, and this is the best he can do. I recommend that you take Nelson's offer."

The deal is made and Nelson, Parkington and Fisher are all reasonably happy. Nelson is getting his house, Parkington has a buyer, and Fisher gets a commission ($8,400 at 6 percent) in addition to the mortgage information fee ($50). In the next few weeks matters became more complex.

- Parkington discovers that another mortgage company had lower interest rates and more liberal qualification standards than First Trumpet. With the other company buyer Nelson would have qualified for a larger mortgage. A bigger mortgage, in turn, would have allowed Nelson to make a higher offer for Parkington's property.
- Buyer Nelson also finds out about the lower rates. With lower rates, his monthly costs would have been smaller and the house would have been more affordable. The more he thought about it, the more Nelson realized that the only reason he used First Trumpet was to gain Fisher's good will and assistance.
- Local attorneys have a field day. Parkington's lawyer sues Fisher because, he claims, the $50 fee received by the broker caused him to recommend a loan that did not offer the best possible terms. The less desirable loan, in turn, restricted the buyer's ability to pay more for Parkington's property. In effect, Parkington's lawyer claims that Fisher was an undisclosed dual agent.
- Not to be outdone, buyer Parkington also hires a lawyer. Parkington's attorney said Fisher had steered Nelson to a single lender and that Parkington had used First Trumpet because he feared he would lose the property if he didn't use the broker's loan system.

It doesn't matter if Fisher is absolutely innocent and all claims against him are dismissed. The important point is that it simply doesn't make sense for a broker to charge a minimal number of dollars for a service that potentially can ruin a deal or bankrupt a company. Antagonizing sellers, irritating buyers, and getting sued are not the way localized, community-based organizations build their reputations. Or their businesses.

CLAIMS

We have now seen that the issue of fees for mortgage loan information is something largely exported from the lending industry into the brokerage community. Brokers must defend their right to earn such fees, but conversely not too many are willing to charge prospective borrowers.

Some brokers, however, exact fees for loan information and services. It is their right to do so, and it is also their right to claim—as most loan sources invariably do claim—that they offer the best deal in town.

The *use* of a computer by itself is not unfair or inappropriate. After all, mortgage information—whether from a computer, brochure, loan officer, or a real estate broker—need not spell out every available loan option. If Cropduster Finance sends out a brochure touting their latest mortgage product, they are surely not obligated to mention that a competing firm down the street has a better program. That's the consumer's job.

What is an issue, and a serious one, are various ploys and claims used to justify one loan service over another, including claims sometimes made for broker-based lending systems. Consider the following:

1. *We have the lowest rates in town.* At any given time there may be several hundred lenders active in a given area. On a particular day, one may have a better rate for a specific program than another, but no lender always has the best rates for comparable programs. Just as important, additional costs to get the features a borrower might want and reasonably expect often skew rate comparisons. The lender who has a lower interest rate but more points and costs is not offering a bargain.

2. *We have more liberal qualification standards.* When asked how higher rates can be justified, one response has been that limited access loan systems often have more liberal qualification standards. This is a remarkably disingenuous response.

Mortgage lenders qualify borrowers in part by looking at the ratio of housing costs to income. As an example, for a typical fixed-rate, 30-year mortgage with 20 percent down, a lender might allow someone to devote 28 percent of their pre-tax income to mortgage principal, mortgage interest, property taxes, and homeowners insurance.

By "more liberal qualification standards" some lenders

mean that instead of 28 percent, they allow borrowers to devote 33 percent of their income to basic housing costs. All things being equal, the more generous qualification standard means that a borrower can obtain a larger mortgage.

No one denies that 33 percent is a bigger figure than 28 percent and therefore a more liberal standard. But this "more liberal" standard does not exist in a vacuum. All things are not equal. First of all, because the interest rate is higher, a more liberal qualification standard is *required* to borrow as much money as a less-pricey source might provide. Secondly, a housing allowance of 33 percent is hardly the most liberal standard around. For example, borrowers who use no-money-down VA financing can devote as much as 45 percent of their income to housing costs. Many lenders use 36, 38, 40 and even 45 percent income ratios to qualify borrowers. There are even lenders who make loans where income is not even considered if the down payment is large enough.

3. *We process loans in just 15 minutes.* Loans can be pre-approved, so fast processing need not be an issue. Where it is an issue, many lenders offer speedy application programs. It should also be said that fast approval programs often do not apply to the self-employed, small corporation owners, or those with substantial partnership interests. Also, some companies charge higher rates for identical loans. If you need or want a mortgage in 15 minutes, it can cost you extra—perhaps thousands of dollars over the loan term.

4. *We can start your loan at five percent below current interest rates.* Such programs are typically available only when accompanied by a large up-front payment. In other words, the payment makes up for the lower initial interest rate.

5. *We have all the loan choices you need.* The most basic idea behind providing computers and loan information to brokers is *not to encourage competition and widespread rate comparisons.* The central purpose is to capture business at the earliest moment in the selling process. While you can find a variety of loan programs with broker-based systems, and sometimes even loan information from a small number of

competing lenders on one computer, the mortgage market includes hundreds of lenders and thousands of financing options. Whatever diversity broker systems may have, no one argues that limited-access systems contain all the loans available in one area—including, perhaps, mortgages with better terms and lower rates than anything offered through a broker.

Given that brokers today generally don't want to be in the mortgage business and that there are no *exclusive* benefits created by obtaining a loan through a real estate office, at the very least prospective borrowers should help the real estate community by carefully shopping for loans. If a broker has the best available deal after all fees and charges are considered, that's great. But you'll never be certain how worthwhile a broker's mortgage offerings might be unless you first check with other loan sources.

MAKING LOAN FEES ACCEPTABLE

Like doctors and lawyers, real estate brokers have an inherent right to itemize their services and separately charge for each. Yet the central value of prospective purchasers to brokers and agents is not the loan fees they may generate, but rather the real estate commissions they represent. Alienate buyers over minor mortgage fees and sale opportunities will decline. Seek payment for information available without charge from other brokers—or from mortgage lenders—and customers will simply go elsewhere.

The entrenched tradition has been that brokers concentrate on brokerage, lenders focus on mortgages, and consumers pay nothing for lending information and advice.

In effect, brokers are supplying the field of battle but the real combatants are lenders. Winners today are measured in terms of additional loan closings and market share, items of interest to lenders, not brokers.

If broker-based loan systems are to succeed, then brokers must develop mortgage information and origination programs that largely benefit *borrowers.* Borrowers, after all, are people who buy houses, and people who buy houses are a necessary link in the chain of events that leads to enhanced sales and higher commissions for the real estate community.

To devise an acceptable loan system brokers must take five steps:

First, the system must be open to any lender willing to supply rates and terms. No special deal for one lender or another.

Second, listing agreements must be revised so that sellers are on notice and agree that brokers may collect a fee from purchasers when they provide mortgage information and services. Also, sellers must be told that other loan sources, including perhaps some with better rates and terms, are freely available to the purchaser.

Third, the sale of a home must *never* require the use of a broker's loan origination system. Borrowers must have absolute discretion to find loans elsewhere.

Fourth, borrowers must be told that when residential brokers represent sellers, any financial information they provide may be transmitted to the broker's principal, the seller. Buyer brokers, of course, do not have this concern.

Fifth, the use—or possible use—of mortgage services provided by a broker should be fully disclosed in every purchase offer.

Brokers and lawyers will have to figure out the details, but the central point is that broker-based loan systems to benefit borrowers are not unthinkable. What is not acceptable, however, is a system that *uses* brokers and *benefits* lenders, an arrangement that raises buyer loan costs, makes homes less salable (because they are more expensive to own), and reduces broker commissions (because high loan costs do not maximize sale opportunities).

13

The Education Illusion

When the issue of education and training arises, few people argue that less is better. We want doctors who went to med school and attorneys who attended law school, but for real estate brokers we have a different and lower set of standards. Forget undergraduate degrees or graduate studies, to become a broker in most states all you need is nine to 12 credit hours of college training and two to three years of experience.

Standards for agents are lower yet. To earn a license in most states you must pass both a course and an exam. Basic licensure courses typically require 45 to 60 clock hours of instruction, an academic load that can frequently be completed in less than two weeks.

Looking at the industry's thin educational requirements may lead to cries for greater academic study, but what objective evidence suggests that competency, compensation, or achievement increase with classroom hours? The agent with many professional designations (and therefore many hours of classroom attendance) may enjoy higher earnings than a beginner, but what underlies such productivity? Is it classroom attendance, experience in the field, or a combination of both? And if success for many agents is jointly based on training and experience, who can say if one factor is more important than another?

Rather than education, success in real estate is often defined by social skills. Many agents find listings and sales among their peers; people met at the company, church or country club ("Of course we'll list with you Todd. After all, you're on the greens committee so you must know all about real estate"). Given such marketplace realities, perhaps charm school offers the best chance for big sales and listings.

Over many years the real estate industry has been accused of price fixing and restraint of trade, but no one ever claimed that unreasonable educational standards were used to discourage competition. In fact, one of the industry's best defenses against restraint-of-trade accusations is that minimal educational standards actually encourage competition. Virtually anyone can enter the real estate business, and many new competitors succeed. When new agents do well and young firms capture big listings, it means that established pros are losing business they might otherwise have had if entry-level barriers were higher.

Entry-level classes are little more than cram courses for state licensure exams. This is *not* to say they are poorly taught, but rather that a large number of complex, difficult subjects must be covered in a short period of time. No one really believes that students can grasp the full implication of such subjects as agency, licensure law, listing agreements, sale contracts, discriminatory actions, and disclosure in just a few hours of introductory instruction.

BACK-UP SYSTEMS

Educational requirements for agents would be entirely unsatisfactory if nothing more was required before they began working, but fortunately a potent safeguard to protect the public interest is in place. Agents must deal through brokers and if an agent acts foolishly, unethically, or illegally, it is the broker who is responsible.

Ask these questions: Who pays if an agent claims that a house can be used for commercial purposes and it can't? Who pays if an agent says a property is not for sale to blacks or Catholics? Who pays if an agent receives a fee to steer buyers to one lender or another? Depending on the facts and circumstances in each case, the broker is likely to face mammoth liabilities.

Working with a broker is thus a package deal. If a seller likes agent Green, broker Reed must be included. It is brokers who are hired, brokers who are responsible for their agents, and if an agent fouls up, it is the broker who is in trouble.

It may take formal classes, weekly meetings, or side-by-side desks with a more experienced agent, but no broker who hopes to remain in business can spring an unprepared agent on the public. Every agent must have a backup, and that backup is the broker.

Not only is there a broker behind every agent, but savvy buyers and sellers will insist on additional protections in the form of what may be called "allied professionals."

Brokers play a central role in pricing, marketing and negotiation, but in a typical deal it is not unusual to also see a variety of professionals who participate in the transaction.

- Attorneys can review contracts, provide closing services, and offer legal advice.
- Buyers have begun to use structural inspectors with increasing frequency. Structural inspectors search for serious or hidden defects and evaluate a home's physical condition. To avoid future claims that they knew about hidden defects, both brokers and sellers commonly encourage the use of a structural inspector.
- If there is a loan, then there will be an appraisal. Appraisers work for lenders, not borrowers, but they do provide some protection for purchasers because if an appraisal is too low, a lender will not finance the deal.
- Surveyors can describe a lot, show where a home is located, and identify any instances where a fence or building is improperly located.
- Termite inspectors will determine if a home is infested with termites or other wood-boring insects and whether the house has been damaged by such insects.

While allied professionals can supply many services there is a catch: In the eagerness to clinch a deal, not every buyer or seller uses specialists, a big mistake if a contract is not carefully written or a defect shows up six months after a sale is closed.

THE CASE FOR TERM LICENSING

One of the most serious issues confronted by the real estate industry is the quest for professionalism. Those inside the industry may have little doubt that they are professionals, but those outside are often less generous in their assessment. Certainly someone who earns his or her living through the sale of property is, at least in a monetary sense, a professional real estate broker or agent. But is brokerage itself a profession?

When you think of a professional, you visualize an individual with advanced educational degrees and prolonged training. Simultaneously, a profession often is characterized by few practitioners.

But compared with such undeniably professional occupations as medicine or law, real estate training is minimal. In fact, the barriers to entry in the profession are so low that more than 2 million people are currently licensed to sell property in the United States. *The problem here is that truly competent individuals—and there are many—are indistinguishable in terms of training, licensure, and status from those who are less competent.* If real estate brokerage is to be recognized as a profession by those outside the industry then general standards must be raised. And the best and most straightforward way to raise standards is through the use of term licensing.

Simply stated, term licensing means that after a certain length of time, licensees must either meet specific standards of training and skill or they stop selling real estate. Period.

As an example, agents might be initially allowed to enter the field with the current 45 to 60-hours of training. However, within five years from the date of licensure or the enactment of a term licensure program, all agents would be required to have taken nine hours of college-level courses (or whatever a state requires) and to have passed the broker's exam. Those who don't qualify as brokers will have to leave the field.

Unlike today's licensing practices, term licensing will require occupational advancement and improvement. No longer can an individual remain perpetually qualified to market property as a result of some ancient and obscure rite of passage. More importantly, we will no longer have the spectacle of a wizened Neanderthal attempting to defend a client's economic interests in a complex, modern society. The deadwood will be gone.

With term licensing a broker's license will be based on experience, training and testing. Such arbitrary and unsound concepts as "full-time" and "active" experience can be dropped in favor of observable tests of competence. (Who is a "full-time" agent anyway? Is it someone who spends 60 hours a week chasing listings inefficiently? Or someone who earns all or the majority of his or her living from brokerage?)

The term licensing process can gradually replace the useless and often disingenuous career markers now used in real estate. In an era of inflation, belonging to the "million dollar club" is neither remarkable nor particularly exclusive. Term licensure offers an alternative system of occupational gradation, one based on evolving and improving levels of skill.

Term licensing also produces several other highly desirable results:

- First, the absolute number of licensees will decline, leaving more business—and more income—for those who remain.
- Second, the ratio of brokers to agents will shift over time. More brokers, individuals licensed to practice their skills independently, will be available to serve the public.
- Third, the image of real estate will be enormously improved.
- Fourth, with term licensure real estate will retain its minimal entry-level standards. Everyone will at least have a chance to test real estate as a career.
- Fifth, tougher standards will justify both professional status and professional incomes.

Real estate brokerage involves the very serious process of representing another person in a real estate transaction. It is a process that should be reserved for only the most competent—something term licensing can encourage and require.

14
Lawyers as Competitors

It is not uncommon to find professions that are both closely related and highly competitive, a description that surely applies to brokers and lawyers.

On a daily basis virtually every brokerage activity is tied closely to legal issues. From agency to zoning, brokers cannot act or react without a fundamental understanding of the rules, regulations, and concepts that govern property transactions.

But since rules and regulations are within a lawyer's territory, there is the issue of just how much brokers need to know and how much knowledge they are allowed to use.

The clearest distinction between brokers and lawyers today involves contracts. Can a broker write a real estate agreement without the help of an attorney? The answer varies by state. In some jurisdictions, brokers can write real estate agreements because such efforts are seen as "incidental" to brokering. Other states take a narrow view and restrict brokers to "simple instruments;" forms where brokers are allowed only to fill in appropriate blanks. A third approach is found in the state of New York, where only lawyers can write real estate contracts.

Education is another distinction between lawyers and brokers. Lawyers who engage in buying and selling property as part of their legal practice are normally not required to have a broker's license. But if an attorney hangs out a shingle reading, "H. Fenwick, Esq., Attorney and Real Estate Broker," then Fenwick typically needs a real estate license.

For Fenwick and other attorneys, obtaining a real estate license is easy. Many states, having rules written by attorneys, allow lawyers to obtain a license by simply taking the standard real estate exam, three years of law school being viewed as a more-than-adequate substitute for real estate classes. No less important, it is difficult to imagine how anyone could take courses in contracts, agency and other subjects, graduate from law school, and then fail a state brokerage test.

So now we see that lawyers have contract-preparation rights often denied to brokers and we also can see how easy it is for attorneys to meet licensure standards. Why then do we not have more lawyers acting as brokers?

Historically, the reason has been that in the general case more money could be made practicing law than offering real estate services. Now, however, changing conditions in the legal profession are making brokerage increasingly attractive.

As of 1980 there were 502,000 attorneys in the United States, a large-enough number but one that mushroomed to 741,000 by 1989, according to the Bureau of Labor Statistics. If one-third of the population is under 18, we then have one lawyer for every 225 adults. In comparison, it is commonly estimated that Japan has one lawyer for each 6,300 adults, a total of just 13,000 attorneys in the entire country.

Are there too many attorneys? At what point will the volume of lawsuits, estates, and corporate charters be insufficient to support the legal population? Will a surplus of lawyers lead to more competition and less compensation within the legal profession?

Those who think this situation can't happen should look at the dental industry. The combination of fluoride and huge numbers of dental school graduates has caused more than a few would–be dentists to reconsider their career choice.

For lawyers, troubling trends can be found not only in their growing numbers, but in other developments as well. Though no one directly mentions the term, discount legal services are now available throughout the country. Advertising by attorneys is commonly seen on television even though it was once banned as "undignified." The days when lawyers were sequestered professionals immune from common competitive forces are gone.

The legal profession's growth has spawned a parallel development: pre-emptive strategies to deter litigation. Living wills, employment contracts, disclosure statements, and prenuptial agreements are all forms of legal preventive maintenance designed to reduce future liability and potential legal costs.

The growing use of in-house counsels can be seen as both pre-emptive and cost-effective. With an in-house lawyer, an organization has a trained specialist whose efforts are not diluted by competing clients and causes.

Another pre-emptive strategy is to settle disputes through binding arbitration. Lawyers can be involved in arbitration representing one side or another, but when arbitration agreements specifically ban awards for legal fees, the zeal to participate in such cases suddenly diminishes.

Competition and pre-emptive strategies lower actual costs and reduce opportunities for litigation. Another approach, reactive attacks on lawyers, is a fast-growing industry of its own that applies the porcupine principle: mess with me and you may win, but it won't be easy, cheap or painless.

Reactive strategies take several forms, none of which are likely to thrill the legal community:

- Suits for legal malpractice, a growth industry beginning to influence lawyers in the same manner that malpractice issues effect physicians, are now so common that attorneys increasingly elect to ignore unpaid legal bills, the fear being that a non-paying client may turn around and claim malpractice. In one malpractice case, a New York law firm paid $40 million to investors hurt by the failure of a major financier.
- Fines against attorneys for frivolous suits. In one hearing that went to the Supreme Court, Rule 11 of the Federal Rules of Civil Procedure was used to justify a $50,000 fine against an attorney for filing a frivolous action. Rule 11 says, essentially, that attorneys must make a "reasonable inquiry" to assure that a bona fide legal or factual basis exists before pursuing a case.
- Suits against attorneys for conflicts of interest. One Mary-

land firm that advised both savings institutions and a quasi-public agency regulating thrifts settled a conflict-of-interest suit by paying $27 million. As firms grow, or as firms become large relative to the communities they serve, the potential for conflict increases.

- Tort reform, including efforts to cap awards, reduce attorney fees, or both is active throughout the country. In many states awards for non-economic damages (pain and suffering) are now limited. Efforts to change or eliminate the notion that someone with a 1-percent liability can be made responsible for an entire judgment are widely supported.

- The fee structure used by the legal profession is changing. In California, where awards for pain and suffering are limited to $250,000, attorney fees are restricted to 40 percent of the first $50,000 and then less and less until only 10 percent of any award above $200,000 can go to a lawyer. In effect, if a defendant is truly entitled to a large award, the judgment is not diminished by high legal fees.

BROKERS OR EMPLOYEES?

The practice of law has always included transportable skills. Given the changing environment within the legal profession, far tougher educational standards than those required for real estate brokerage, plus an unfettered right to produce contracts, why shouldn't more lawyers become active as brokers?

Lawyers already play a highly visible role in commercial brokerage, which is where the most complexity and the largest commissions can be found. Residential brokerage may be next, especially among top-of-the-line properties.

Brokerage can be seen as both a business and as a marketing tool for attorneys. Not only can lawyers represent buyers and sellers, but whoever walks in the door is also a possible candidate for leases, wills, divorces, and corporate work even if they never buy or sell a property.

While it seems likely that more attorneys will become active in real estate, possession of a law degree by itself will not assure success. Profitable brokerage is an entrepreneurial activity that requires more than course credits or framed certificates. Law-

Should Brokerage Fees Be Public?

For several years the legal community has been pushing "model" legislation that would make public the sale prices in all single-family real estate transactions. This is already done in most states, but in some jurisdictions sale prices are confidential, which makes pricing, assessments, and taxation difficult.

The model legislation also requires the public reporting of brokerage fees, the apparent theory being that such commissions are an important part of sale arrangements.

If enacted, such legislation would represent a serious setback to real estate competition. MLS networks once required listing brokers to include full commission rates when entering properties into the system, publication that often produced peer pressure and price uniformity. Most—and probably all—MLS systems now list only co-op fees for selling brokers, a system that keeps private the total commission arrangements between listing brokers and sellers.

Interestingly enough, the lawyers' proposal does not suggest recording legal fees associated with a home sale.

yers, like brokers, will have to fight for every listing and sale. Equally important, trends influencing the legal profession will create new options for brokers.

As long as law schools continue to churn out tens of thousands new graduates each year to join the vast army of lawyers already in practice, the surplus of legal talent will continue to grow. This surplus will allow brokers to go out, hire an attorney, provide a desk, and thus have on-site legal counsel paid with an annual salary. Certainly a company with 40 or 50 brokers generates a sufficient volume of legal work to justify such employment. Or, several smaller brokers can get together, hire a full-time lawyer and apportion costs according to usage.

Another strategy might work somewhat like 1-hour optical services that have on-site optometrists. Brokers would supply space to attorneys with rent related to revenues—the greater

the attorney's income the larger the monthly rent. In this way
the broker can have access to legal services while effectively
profiting from a lawyer's non-brokerage work.

Attorneys, especially those without established practices,
may find this concept attractive because they will obtain both
space and an immediate source of business, something not to be
overlooked as thousands of new lawyers join the workforce each
month.

15
Winners and Losers

Ten years ago uniformity defined the brokerage industry: one commission schedule, one marketing concept, one deal for agents, and no representation for purchasers. New competitive forces have now been unleashed, and with such pressures buyers and sellers will have more choices, traditional brokers will face new competitors, and successful agents will have more alternatives than in the past.

In looking toward the future there will be winners and losers, sometimes for the strangest reasons.

Take the bedrock issue of commissions.

The old days of uniform commissions are dead. The consumerist's ideal of negotiated fees will become increasingly common, but guess what: "negotiated" is not the same as "lower."

Competition means not only that brokers will fight for listings and sales, it also means that owners will compete for brokerage services. If brokers are going to stay in business they will simply have to become more selective. The owner with a salable house will be able to strike a better deal than the owner who has failed to maintain his property. Poorly located homes and properties with unrealistic selling prices represent more risk to brokers and will cost more to sell.

Homes that are poorly maintained, badly located or overpriced always cost more to sell. The difference is that in the past other sellers effectively subsidized such sales. In time to come, those with attractive properties will benefit, and those with less

salable properties will pay the higher fees they should always
have paid.

FEWER AGENTS, MORE BROKERS

The tradition in real estate has always been that a vast number
of agents were good for the industry, a tradition that makes
increasingly less sense. With tighter margins traditional brokers
can no longer afford the training, hand-holding and desk costs
associated with entry-level and unproductive agents. Since
agents can only practice when they are affiliated with a broker,
so tougher broker standards for agents will effectively eliminate
marginal agents from the marketplace with greater speed than
in the past. Most importantly, to preserve bottom-line margins,
brokers will negotiate smaller splits with new agents and those
who are unproductive.

Fewer agents will impact several concerned parties. As less
people enter real estate, the need for licensure courses and
exams will decline. Professional organizations will have fewer
members, but perhaps the members who remain will be more
active. States will collect less money because the number of
agents will drop.

Although there will be fewer agents, the number of brokers
will increase. The cost of entering the real estate business is so
small that with only a few deals each year a broker can at least
break even. Cottage industry brokerage—an amalgam of
cheaper technology and home offices—will create new opportunities for those who wish to function as sole practitioners or
to operate small firms.

OPENING UP THE MLS

Until recently, only exclusive-right-to-sell listing agreements
could be used to enter properties into a local MLS. A growing
number of MLS networks now permit exclusive agency agreements, listing contracts that allow owners to market their
homes independently and not pay a fee if they sell directly
without a broker.

While more MLS networks are likely to allow exclusive
agency listings, brokers have little incentive to push for such
arrangements. On one hand, traditional brokers are hired pre-

cisely because owners do not want to sell properties by themselves. On the other, flat-fee and discount brokers cannot use exclusive agency agreements because owners often show homes directly.

The following changes seem likely in future MLS networks.

First, standardized listing agreements will be changed to provide three commission arrangements.

- If the property is listed and sold by one broker, the broker will get a full fee.
- If a property is listed by one broker and sold by a selling broker, the two brokers will divide the fee.
- If a property is listed by one broker and a buyer broker represents a purchaser, then the listing broker will receive a full commission less a co-op fee. At closing, the buyers will receive a credit equal to the co-op amount and from this credit, buyers may then turn around and pay the buyer broker. If the amount of the credit is more than the buyer broker's fee, then purchasers will pocket the difference. If the credit is less than the amount owed to a buyer representative, then purchasers must pay the additional cost from their own funds.

Second, if MLS systems can list properties, why not list purchasers? A broker with an exclusive-right-to-buy arrangement can surely tell other brokers that a purchaser is looking for a property in a particular area and with specific characteristics.

Third, MLS systems will increasingly include other services. For example, a photo of every house in a community along with tax and appraisal information would make the system far more valuable. An MLS might also carry loan information, providing all lenders have equal access to the system. One advantage with such systems is that they can be programmed to automatically convert rates and points to the annual percentage rate (APR) so that loans are readily comparable.

RELOCATION

We are a mobile people and with mobility comes the need to find housing in new areas. Relocation is a $15 billion industry that helps purchasers find new homes, but with a catch: relocation brokers are commonly paid by sellers.

Thus we can easily have a situation where Mr. Boyles moves to a new town, is not familiar with prices, neighborhoods, schools or commuting, and then depends upon a seller's representative for information, contract forms and recommendations. Good news for a seller, perhaps not so good for Mr. Boyles.

One can envision a different concept, one where relocation services act as buyer agents. Such a relationship is more logical than the current system, but it is also less likely to attract broker interest.

The largest real estate firms now use seller-oriented relocation services, a position that makes sense because all large firms also act as seller agencies. For them to switch to pro-buyer relocators seems unlikely because local firms that handle relocations would then be in the implausible position of representing both local homeowners and out-of-town buyers.

Rather than replacing the current system of relocation networks with local broker representatives, a more likely scenario is that parallel buyer networks will emerge, seek local broker representation, and then pursue corporate housing clients. Corporations want to reduce relocation costs, so the ability to engage a local buyer representative will be attractive.

If buyer-oriented relocation services develop into a strong market force, brokers with large relocation services today will be minimally affected. Out-of-town buyers will purchase something, and what they purchase is likely to come from brokers with something to sell.

MIXED FEE BROKERAGE

Today's real estate companies tend to fall into certain categories. There are traditional, discount, and flat-fee firms representing either buyers or sellers. Agents are hired on a traditional, 100-percent, or employee basis. What we don't have is a realty supermarket that offers a complete menu of services as well as several commission arrangements for agents.

A realty supermarket seems feasible providing it serves either buyers or sellers, but not both. Within the company there might be consultants who work with flat-fee clients and agents who offer a full package of services. Full services will be available at a discount in those instances where properties are particularly salable and therefore less risky to the broker. Premium prices will be charged for hard-to-sell homes, the theory being more business risk requires more potential reward.

Paying agents according to different fee schedules is no more difficult than setting up a computer spreadsheet for each agent, entering their fee arrangement, and sending out the right check.

A realty supermarket might have 50 agents—10 agents on a 100-percent fee schedule, and 40 paid on performance. If a 100-percenter is required to pay $1,500 a month, then the broker will have $180,000 coming in the door each year in addition to fee splits with other agents.

Realty supermarkets will allow brokers to compete with discount and flat fee firms, to have income even when sales are slow, to place agents in positions that best use their talents, and to vie with 100-percent firms for top producers. In addition, realty supermarkets will include a full-time loan adviser, an attorney, and an insurance broker.

The loan advisor will provide financing assistance to buyers and sellers. His or her compensation will be a salary plus a bonus based on the number or value of transactions completed each month. No money will be paid to the loan advisor by a lender, thus assuring that the loan advisor's only interest is making deals work.

An attorney can either be employed by a realty supermarket or simply housed next to its offices. Paid a flat fee per transaction, the lawyer will work on the broker's behalf to review all offers, provide legal advice, and write special clauses.

An insurance broker can operate on-site and pay rent for the use of space, equipment and facilities. Buyers will be told up front and in writing that they have the right to purchase insurance from any source, but as a matter of convenience there is an insurance broker in the office. Many brokers now sell insurance and an agent on-site will simply formalize an ongoing industry practice.

While a one-office realty supermarket seems workable, a more likely scenario has several brokers in a metropolitan area getting together and opening a chain of supermarket offices with a single name, or a large firm converting offices to a supermarket arrangement. More offices will give brokers better name recognition, allow for the purchase of advertising at lower rates and permit the establishment of a single training center with a common group of courses.

A BETTER DEAL FOR SELLERS

The changing world of brokerage will provide new opportunities for homeowners, particularly those with good properties. There is no doubt that a wide choice of brokerage services will be available in virtually all communities. Flat-fee, discount and traditional brokers will all vie for business, competition that can only help consumers.

Fees are likely to remain relatively constant when compared with today's rates, but the average disguises variable commissions. Those with attractive homes and a willingness to bargain will earn lower rates, and those with hard-to-sell properties will pay more.

FISBOs will be part of the market, but fewer sales are likely to be conducted entirely without a broker. The growing number of flat-fee and discount brokers will erode the price issue that bothers so many self-sellers.

BETTER DEALS FOR BUYERS

No group will see more profound changes in the real estate marketing system than buyers. The important point is not that buyer brokerage will become widespread, but rather that buyers will become more aware of marketplace realities.

Agency disclosure statements, now used in more than 30 states, will be used in all jurisdictions. While buyers can obtain basic information from listing and selling brokers, when it comes time to develop an offer, they will increasingly use buyer agents, attorneys, and structural inspectors to improve their bargaining position.

As to buyer brokers generally, they are destined to become more numerous, particularly in major metropolitan areas and among relocation services. Still, being "more numerous" is a relative concept. There are few brokers who actively promote buyer representation today, and fewer still who serve buyers to the exclusion of sellers.

FINANCING

Except for the rich, real estate deals are unworkable without financing. The S&L crisis and problems with VA, FHA and commercial banks have all raised questions concerning where mortgage money will be found in the future.

There is little doubt that the VA and FHA programs face revision. Larger insurance premiums will undoubtedly be proposed, especially for deals that involve little money down. The trouble with tougher FHA and VA requirements is that such federal programs are specifically designed to provide mortgage loan guarantees for borrowers who might otherwise not qualify for conventional loans. Raise up-front costs and down payment requirements and the people who suffer most are those individuals least likely to find mortgage funds anywhere else. By creating stiffer requirements it will be possible to effectively gut the FHA and VA programs, something supported by those who believe government should not compete with private business in any field.

The good news is that a major new source of financing will undoubtedly open up. Each year billions of dollars are stashed away in small and large pension funds and over time such accounts have grown untaxed until they incorporate a major share of our national wealth. Instead of investing in stocks, bonds and fervent prayer, pension managers and trustees will increasingly allocate some portion of their assets to mortgages.

As to the issue of brokers originating loans and receiving fees for mortgage work, brokers will undoubtedly provide more financial information to buyers. The financial systems used by brokers—unlike many of today's systems—will be competitively neutral so that mortgage programs will have to stand on their merits and no loan source will have a built-in advantage.

In the future, the odds are that with appropriate and informed disclosure to both buyers and sellers, some brokers will offer financial services. Others will ultimately decide that while charging for loans is both feasible and allowable, it's simply better to concentrate on making deals.

PART III
Other Views, Other Voices

How has the real estate industry evolved in the past decade? Where does it go from here?

To obtain a broader view of the marketplace than one writer can possibly provide, we spoke with leading figures in the real estate community, individuals whose ideas influence millions of home sales each year.

Within the interviews that follow readers will discover insight, shared views, disagreement and conflict. There are small and large debates concerning almost every issue, a healthy sign that reflects the ongoing competition that now dominates the real estate industry.

The interviews were conducted individually, taped, and then edited. Each participant had a chance to review and comment on his or her edited transcript, but not anyone else's interview or any of the material found elsewhere in this book.

Participation in this book does not imply, infer, or suggest an endorsement of this guide by any of those interviewed or the organizations with which they are affiliated. Instead, participation should be seen for no more than it is, a willingness to answer questions and test ideas.

HARLEY E. ROUDA
1991 President
National Association of Realtors
Chicago, Illinois

He majored in accounting at Ohio State University, but Harley E. Rouda thought real estate might offer more opportunities than ledgers and trial balances. Beginning with a single office in 1956 in Columbus, Ohio, Rouda's company, HER, Inc., is now the largest real estate organization in central Ohio, a firm with 23 offices and 452 agents that handles more than 5,000 transactions a year.

Rouda is also the 1991 president of the National Association of Realtors (NAR), the largest real estate organization in the country and a powerful presence in Washington. Courtly and direct, Rouda has a keen grasp of both association interests and bottom-line economics.

Question: What changes will emerge within real estate during the coming decade?
It used to be a very simple business—10 or 15 years ago. You wrote an offer on a piece of property and closed it in ten days or two weeks. Now it takes 30 days if you're lucky, more like 45 days. Paperwork and government regulations have made our business very complicated.

Every time we turn around there is more legislation affecting how you list and sell real estate, especially at the state and local level. It's become a far more complicated business than in the past and people entering the field will need more training and education to keep up.

Question: Around the country we have about two million people with real estate licenses. Is that too many?
Not really. I think there is an old adage that of all the real estate salespeople, about 20 percent of them do 80 percent of the business. Certainly if you have two million licensees, there are 400,000 getting the job done. The rest of them are in and out like a yo-yo.

When times are good people flock to the real estate business. When times are so-so they kind of hang around. When times get bad, they get out.

Question: Is the estimate of a 20-percent turnover among agents fair?

I don't have that figure. I know in our company it's about 10 or 12 percent, but it is usually about 10 or 12 percent that we ask to leave because they just are not producing. I probably should add that we believe only in full-time real estate sales associates. We don't have part-time people. It's against my philosophy.

Question: In most states you can obtain an agent's license with 45 to 60 clock hours of training. Is that enough?

Well, for an entry-level agent, I'm not too sure it has to go beyond that. A lot of states have continuing education. In Ohio, where I'm from, we have 30 hours every three years. In that 30 hours we have to take three hours of law and three hours of civil rights for housing. So with those six hours locked in plus the other 24 hours, we are on a continuous educational program.

I will tell you this, when continuing education first started in Ohio, it was pretty bad. But now you better have a good course or it will not be allowed, so consequently we are getting a very good education and Ohio is not alone.

Question: You have only full-time associates. What is a full-time associate anyway? Should real estate licenses be restricted to full-time brokers and agents?

I'm not too sure you can define a full-time associate. I don't think you can define a real estate associate by the hours they put in.

I know people who spend 40 hours a week in the real estate business and make $100,000. I know people who spend 60 hours a week and make $15,000. Well, they both work full-time, but one is very successful because they are good, the other one is less successful because they are not so good. They just don't have it. So I don't think you can put an hour on it. In our company, we look at a dollar amount and it varies by office and the price of homes being sold.

But I have to address your question, because you really asked, "Should we allow part-time people in real estate?" I'm not an attorney, although I feel like I am when I deal so much with the terms in our business, but I think right off the top it would almost be like a restraint of employment if you told someone they couldn't come into a business unless they were full-time.

If you took that position, that would sure cover everybody including doctors, lawyers, and Indian chiefs. I don't think there's a regulatory agency anywhere that would allow that to happen.

Question: Real estate traditionally has been characterized by large numbers of smaller firms, individual offices with fewer than 10 agents. Do you think that's the trend of the future or will we see larger firms enjoying a greater market share?

It depends on where you go. If you are talking about a major metro area, there will always be large firms there. Large conglomerates don't go to small and medium-sized towns, so there isn't dominance in such communities by any one firm. There are just a lot of small firms and that's really the bulk of the real estate business—the small firms. I think they comprise some 70 percent of our total business nationwide.

One large company from outside the real estate industry said in 1978 that they were going to buy 50 regional firms to form a national real estate network. They wanted to buy my company, but I wasn't selling.

That was the start of the conglomerates coming into our industry. Those companies that bought real estate firms found out that real estate people are great entrepreneurs, that their purchase really can't work and they can't be successful unless they have that entrepreneurial feeling within the firm.

We found in most places that owners who sold to conglomerates stayed on for about three years as managers or consultants and then left. As the original owners left, business generally would drop off.

I don't think there will be too many more big companies coming on the scene. I think, I hate to say this, but I think Wall Street has learned its lessons, that the real estate commissions that looked so healthy to them in the past can't be worked by people other than real estate entrepreneurs.

Question: In recent years we have seen the growth of the 100-percent commission broker. How do they affect the real estate community?

In 1983 across the country, the bottom line for brokers was probably around 42–43 percent of gross commissions received. So if you had $1,000 come in on a real estate sale, the company ended up with about $425. That has slowly eroded. In our own company, three years ago, we were at 42.5 percent. We are now down to 38 percent and I was bemoaning that fact to some of my compatriots around the country until I found out that they are running between 30–35 percent, so I feel pretty good.

But the company dollar has been going down and there is absolutely no doubt that the 100-percent concept has caused real estate companies, large and small, to pay sales associates more money. I don't think it will continue to erode much more, but I would say that the broker's bottom line has really taken a beating in the last three or four years because of the 100-percent concept.

Question: Can a firm such as yours and other firms survive with reduced ratios?

If you are a good business man or woman, I think you'll survive in any market condition. I've lived through five real estate recessions since I started in 1953. Yes, you can survive.

We are a large company, there is no question about it. We closed $478 million worth of property in 1989. But in 1988 and 1989, our total expenses for those two years increased 2.7 percent over 1987.

Question: So you held down costs?

You've got it. Because we are paying the sales people so much more money, we've got to start cutting to maintain the bottom line.

Question: What steps did you take to cut that bottom line?

We consolidated two offices and where we had three people

doing the job, we would hire two and a part-timer. We cut our supply budget in half and postage, which was one percent of our gross expenses, was knocked down to half a percent.

Question: In addition to 100-percent brokers, full-service firms are also challenged by discount and flat-fee brokers. How have they influenced your business?
They have already reached good proportions in some areas. I would think that the concept would be very intriguing to people when you are in a very strong market, but oddly enough, they are making some great impact in areas where it is very difficult to sell homes, in what I would call recessionary markets.

Question: Does that make it tough for a firm like yours?
It would be tough if they had an impact in Columbus, sure, because it is going to affect your bottom line.

But also bear in mind that from what I've been able to gather, they do not offer the services of a full-service broker and not every home can be sold without that full service.

They don't seem to have a strong referral base for out-of-town buyers, so if you're in a market where you have transient people coming into your town and you don't have access to those people, sale opportunities are lost.

Also, a lot of the discount brokers, and that's what they call themselves, or some call them that, rarely show the property. In most cases the seller shows the property. We advise all our sellers that if humanly possible, when the property is shown, get out, because the agent can better answer the questions that buyers may have.

From what we've been able to see, most of their marketing techniques are diametrically opposed to traditional real estate marketing practices. I think in the long run, sellers will be hurt trying to get their homes sold with discount firms.

Question: Does your company represent only sellers?
We are strictly a sellers' agency.

Question: If buyer Smith comes to you and has a buyer broker, what happens?

The buyer broker shows the property and hopes he sells it.

Question: So, in other words, your policy is, fine. You are interested in selling the house, not whether a buyer broker is or is not involved?

There is no issue. I will tell you this. We do not pay them the same fee that we pay a sub-agent of the seller.

Question: You would pay them a fee?

Oh yes. With a sellers' permission.

Question: Why should you pay a buyer broker? You represent the seller. Wouldn't a buyer broker want to distance himself from the seller's representative and charge a fee separately?

That's utopian, the way it should be done. That's not what's being done.

Buyer brokerage is not new. As long as I've been in the business, commercial brokers have been involved in buyer brokerage. They have a client and they say, "I'll represent you in Columbus, Ohio." And they get a fee, and there's no problem. Residential buyer brokerage has just come about the last couple years. Historically, the residential buyer has rarely, if ever, paid a real estate commission. So for all the years people have been buying and selling property, the residential seller paid a real estate commission.

Now, because of buyer brokers, someone is saying "Hey Mr. Buyer, you work with me and I want a fee." Buyers are not educated about this. It's foreign to them. They don't understand it.

So as a result you have to make sure you do not discourage the buyer broker from showing your property. That's number one.

But number two, when we list a property, and I assume most people do the same thing, you've got to point out to your sellers that they are going to pay us a commission. And we, Mr. and Mrs. Seller, would like to take a portion of that commission and give it to a buyer broker to entice them to show the property.

But we want you to understand, Mr. and Mrs. Seller, that buyer brokers have an adversarial role. They are not going to represent you, but yet if you allow us, we will pay them.

Question: Have you had buyer brokers come to you and say, "I don't want anything from you, the buyer is paying me?"

We had more than 5300 closings last year, and of those 25 were buyer broker deals. Of the 25, 15 were with real estate sales associates from other companies buying for themselves or a relative. We had 10 true buyer broker transactions out of 5300 closings and each one received a fee from the seller through us.

Question: If a seller said to you, "I want you to sell my home, but I don't want you to show it to anybody represented by a buyer broker," what happens then? Does the seller have a right to determine who represents the purchaser?

No. But they can refuse to allow us to pay a buyer broker any money from our commission on the sale. That's all sellers can do.

Question: Do you care if a buyer broker uses a lock box?

No, as long as somebody sells the property.

Question: We have more than a thousand MLS systems in the country. The majority of them are based on agency/sub-agency relationships. Some are not. Could you have a functioning, effective MLS system without agency/sub-agency, as has been proposed in New York state?

In effect, for years we had just that. That is really how we operated. There was no such thing as sub-agency.

Question: In the state of Ohio?

No, in the whole country. We didn't have sub-agency or buyer brokerage, we just had cooperating brokers. There was no defined sub-agency.

I think the feeling of most real estate people, the vast majority if not almost all real estate people, was that if you had Mr. and Mrs. Jones as buyer clients—I didn't say custom-ers—clients, you treated them as your clients all the way through and you represented them to the very best of your ability. And if I happened to have a listing with Mr. and Mrs. Brown, I represented them.

This worked and worked very well and rarely did we have a problem until the legal profession, in its wisdom, determined that as a broker helping the buyer you were really a sub-agent of the seller, because when the seller paid a commission to me, I took part of that commission and gave it to you. Because you received part of the commission, you are precluded from giving anything to the buyer that would put the seller in a disadvantaged position.

Until that happened, we had a relatively simple business and I think, generally speaking, the vast majority of buyers and sellers were treated very fairly.

Question: If New York or any other state were, in fact, to pose a situation where sub-agency was no longer permitted, would there be a radical change in the business again?

First of all, let's hope they don't. If they did that, we would go back to what I just described or you'd have to have a law that says you must either be a buyer broker or you must be a seller broker.

If that happens, it will be very difficult for a single company to be both. Large firms, it just seems to me as a practical matter, can either be seller representatives or buyer representatives. It would be very difficult for a large firm to have both one office that represents sellers and another office down the street to represent buyers.

Question: Could you see two separate corporations with common ownership?

Yes, with common ownership, but with a different broker in each company who is responsible to the buyer broker and another one who is responsible to the seller broker.

I am the broker of record of my company. We only represent sellers. If we formed a separate company and I owned part of it and was the broker of record, if there was ever a suit between the two companies, how could I be on each side? There would have to be a different broker of record who would be responsible for the buyer brokers within that company, as I am responsible for the seller brokers in my company.

Question: Traditionally, MLS systems have been run by the real estate community. We now live in an era of computers and high tech. What is to prevent a large corporation or union, or simply a corporation that sets itself up to do this, from forming its own alternative MLS system? What if someone not in the brokerage community says, "Look, this is a great business. I'm going to start a housing information service known as Ralph's Multiple Listing Service."
Why not?

Question: Is that possible?
Absolutely.

Question: For the record, does NAR believe that brokerage fees, commissions, and charges are absolutely negotiable?
They are absolutely negotiable.

Question: Suppose I list my property for $200,000 with a commission of "x" percent and I receive an offer for $180,000. Why can't I turn around and say to the broker, "I'll take $180,000 if you'll take a lower fee?"
Our exclusive listing contract is very clear. It says that you, the seller, will pay a certain fee if we obtain a valid offer at the listed price, or any other price or term that is agreeable. A provision for a fee at the lower sale price is already built in, so if the commission becomes negotiable, it is because the real estate agent has allowed it to become negotiable.

Question: Conceivably a seller could say, "Look you've brought me $180,000, but you know I really want $200,000. I'll take $180,000 if you'll take a lower fee." What happens then?
I'd say the sales associate, the agent, has the right to accept or reject the seller's offer.

Question: Since the listing contract is really an agreement between a broker and a seller, would the sales associate or the broker make that decision?

It's the broker's contract with the seller. Most sales people are very astute when it comes to negotiation. The first thing they say is "Gee, I'd like to do it, but I have no right to do that. I'll have to talk to my broker."

Now if the sales person is real smart, he or she says, "OK Bill, you're going to take the $180,000 but you want to pay us a smaller fee for our work. Let's counter at a higher price and then we'll both be happy."

Question: As the practice of real estate brokerage becomes more complex, and as attorneys run out of people to sue, do you think we'll see increasing numbers of attorneys turning to the practice of real estate brokerage?

I would hope that we are a good enough industry so that they'd starve if they did. If the real estate companies are doing the kind of job they should be doing, really and truly it shouldn't be a problem.

Question: Many jurisdictions now require all brokers to provide state-mandated disclosure statements to buyers explaining that the broker works for a seller unless otherwise stated. Such disclosure forms have greatly reduced so-called "dual agency" suits against brokers. Are there any other disclosure forms that have cut broker liability?

Most suits evolve because something happens to the house. The seller takes the drapes, or there's water in the basement, or the roof leaks, or a window breaks, something.

In California, the real estate agent and the seller complete a disclosure statement, signed by the seller, that accompanies a contract all the way through to closing. As a result, suits against real estate people have been cut by something like 70 percent.

Question: There are approximately two million brokers and agents in the country. Eight hundred thousand belong to NAR. In 1989, 26.1 percent of the people in NAR contributed to RPAC, the political action committee sponsored by the organized real estate community. Does RPAC have enough support to be effective in Washington?

Well, we're the third-largest fundraiser on Capitol Hill and

26 percent is really not all that bad. I've worked on church fundraisers so I know that's not too bad.

Just remember one thing, contributions to congressional candidates do absolutely nothing but get you in the door to say "Hello." It gives you an opportunity to tell your side of the story. I don't believe that the amount of money that a congressman or senator can receive under current law is ever going to cause a vote to swing one way or the other. It is not going to happen.

All it does is open the door. If our argument is logical, I think we have an opportunity to at least have them listen objectively to what we have to say.

Question: There is considerable debate about the question of referral fees. NAR has come out against so-called naked referral fees. What do you do in your company with referral fees for loans or fees for loan information?

Our company does not collect any referral fees, or fees for providing loan information.

Question: And your agents?

If we found someone who wanted to charge a fee, we'd tell him or her to cease and desist.

GAIL LYONS
Broker-Owner
Boulder Real Estate Services, Ltd.
Boulder, Colorado

Few subjects raise more questions within real estate than buyer agency. Why are buyers largely unrepresented today? Should they be represented? If buyers are represented, how should brokers charge for their services?

Gail Lyons has been in the real estate business since 1973, offered buyer agency services for many years, and has lectured with partner Don Harlan on the subject to real estate groups nationwide. She is a past president of the Colorado Association of Realtors, a director of the National Association of Realtors, and co-author, with Harlan, of *Buyer Agency: Your Competitive Edge in Real Estate.*

Question. If two people get divorced and the divorce is contested, each side typically has an attorney. In real estate, when there's a transaction, you have a buyer with one set of interests and a seller with conflicting demands, yet they rarely have separate representatives. Why?
Many times they have different representation. I always do it that way.

Question. But you specifically hold yourself out as a broker who offers buyer representation. Is that typical around the country?
It's becoming a lot more typical. In the Colorado area I guess 25 percent of the business is done by buyer agents.

Boulder is a very unique community so I don't think any judgment should be made for the rest of the nation, but buyer agency has definitely caught on here.

Around the country, from what we've seen, probably 10 to 15 percent of all transactions involve buyer agency unless you're in California or Hawaii.

Question. Do you think it's higher or lower in those areas?
Well, a California survey shows that 92 percent of all agents who co-op have acted as buyer agents at least once.

Question. When you're engaged as a buyer's broker, who pays your fee?

In terms of my buyer agency contract, my fee is the responsibility of the buyer, however it comes out of the transaction almost exclusively. Remember that every transaction is a combination of the seller's equity and the buyer's money, so the transaction proceeds should pay both listing and selling agents' fees.

Question. Let's say that I'm representing a seller and I'm going to get a 6-percent fee, but you represent a purchaser, do I still get a 6-percent fee?

Usually not in my market.

Question. What if I say to the seller, "Look, we have a pre-existing listing agreement. It says I am to receive a 6-percent fee and I don't want to take anything less."

We have seen it happen around the country, especially in markets where buyer agency is infrequent. It's called double-dipping and it's something that should be discouraged. Double dipping is when the listing agent receives a "full" listing commission, refuses to co-op with a buyer's agent and the buyer's agent is paid his fee directly by the purchaser. The combined fees then equal about 1.5 times what is customary in the market.

Question. But don't I have the right to have my listing agreement with the seller honored?

Absolutely you have the right to that.

Question. Does the FHA or VA allow mortgage funds to be used to underwrite buyer brokerage fees?

The VA says if there is a buyer agent involved, the buyer cannot pay the agent's fee, the fee must be paid by the seller.

In Colorado and many other states that I've worked in, the FHA allows the payment by either the seller or the buyer of the buyer agent's fee and it can be financed. It's part of the transaction just like loan discount points.

Question. Suppose you're a buyer agent and a property has been listed with a 2-percent commission. Suppose also that your buyer agent fee is 3 percent. What happens at closing?

My buyer contract states my fee and that I will look first to the transaction for my commission. If I can't get all of it out of the transaction, then the buyer will be personally responsible for the remainder and must pay me at closing.

Question. If there's a slump in the local community, and sellers can't sell their houses, I can go in and negotiate with anybody and they will be elated to accept whatever I want to pay. Why do I need a buyer broker if I'm in a buyer's market?

Most buyers don't have the expertise to do that and need assistance. There's also a lot more to a transaction than just price. Between contract and closing these days we go through all kinds of additional legal work and inspections that we didn't used to do, and each one tends to reopen the contract and reopen negotiations. Buyers really need to have a professional work for them.

Question. Do a large percentage of your transactions now involve structural inspectors?

I can't think of a contract in the last three years that has not had an inspection.

Question. As a buyer representative, you cannot be a subagent. How do you deal with your local MLS?

All listings in our MLS offer subagency, they must. However, most listing agents will cooperate with buyer agents and pay a fee. Our MLS offers what is called the "MLS Plus" concept, which means listing agents can offer separate co-op fees for subagents and for buyer agents. The co-op fees need not be the same under this system.

Question. Can a selling broker refuse to divide a fee with a buyer broker?

If that's in the listing contract, that's correct.

Question. Do you also represent sellers?

Absolutely.

Question. What happens if buyer Smith, who is your client, wants to buy only one property in the world and it's owned by seller Jones, who is also your client?

When I take either a listing contract or a buyer agency contract, I disclose to my buyers and my sellers that because I take both listings and buyer clients, there's always the possibility that a buyer client might want to purchase a seller client's property. If that happens, I would be a dual agent and I disclose that possibility to them at the time of listing. If such a transaction actually takes place, then a dual agency agreement is negotiated and all parties agree to certain terms. Buyers and sellers also have the option of terminating their agreement with me if they don't want to go through with the dual agency.

Question. Let's say that I was the buyer in this case and I didn't want to have a dual agency relationship but I've already told you information about my financial capacity. Would you give that information to a seller?

It's a very difficult position.

Question. Have you ever had this situation?

No.

Question. Can big firms, those with a large proportion of all local listings, engage in buyer representation?

The only way that a large firm can do buyer agency is if it will allow dual agency for in-house sales. A dual agency in which you're selling your own listing is next to impossible because it's very difficult to fully represent both sides. However, where you have a broker who is the dual agent, but you also have Agent A working with the seller and Agent B with the buyer, that works quite well and can be done with full disclosure and informed consent.

Question. But isn't the same broker on both sides of the deal?

The broker is a dual agent, but in practice, if you go into a large company, it is very rare that the broker gets personally involved with or even knows very much about individual buyers and sellers.

Question. It's not the agents who have relationships with buyers and sellers, it's agents who have relationships under the authority of a broker. Correct?

Absolutely, but on the practical side, we're finding that if large companies are doing buyer agency and they've got listings, they've got to provide for the possibility of dual agency because it may occur. It's the broker who's the dual agent but individual selling and listing agents can still work very, very confidentially with their buyer client or a seller client.

Question. What happens if a large company has a buyer client and a seller client and they have a conflict that winds up in arbitration or in court. Will the broker be caught in the middle?

Absolutely, no question about it. However, you've got to recognize that disclosed dual agency is a whole lot safer than the undisclosed dual agency that many people are unintentionally doing today.

Question. Imagine this situation. Agent Smith has helped somebody sell a house. They're very happy with him, so they ask Smith to help them find a new home. Is he an undisclosed dual agent?

If Smith is working as a subagent, he may well be an undisclosed dual agent because agents working with buyers get to know them very, very well. And even though they are subagents for sellers, their actions, their words and their behavior can lead buyers to believe that they are being represented by broker Smith. This is especially true when the buyer, as in this case, is a former seller. The best way to avoid the problem is for Smith to be a buyer's agent.

Question. Suppose I list a property and an agent for another firm brings a potential buyer to my open house and explains— incorrectly—that, "Yes, sure you can have a commercial kennel in this neighborhood." Are there circumstances where I can be held liable for the agent's remarks?

Oh, horrendous liability.

Question. And the seller too?
Absolutely.

Question. Is the liability issue one reason to step away from subagency?
Yes, that's one of the things of which people are becoming more aware. It started in Hawaii. The sellers over there just plain don't want the liability because they have no control over subagents who could be saying or doing anything.

Question. If we move to a cooperative system, how will that change brokerage operations around the country?
To me that's really what we have. Most of the transactions, I don't care where you are in the country, most of the transactions are not strongly adversarial. Yes, the buyer wants the lowest price, and, yes, the seller wants the highest price, but in order to get a contract, they've got to come to agreement and that's the object of negotiation. It isn't like a lawsuit where you've got a plaintiff and a defendant and you're totally on opposite sides.

Question. But shouldn't brokers be advocates?
If you're an agent, that's one of the things you need to be trained to do and advocacy is one of the things I do.

Question. When you give buyer agency seminars around the country, are they typically sponsored by local brokerage groups?
They're usually sponsored by either local or state associations. We've worked for large independents, we've worked for franchises, and we've acted as consultants to firms that want to implement buyer agency or even the correct practice of dual agency.

Question. Is it fair to say that five years ago they probably wouldn't have had you?
That's probably right.

Question. Why the change?
I think disclosure laws have made everybody a whole lot more sensitive to the issue. That and a number of lawsuits

that have occurred around the country have sensitized people to the fact that real estate licensees have always been agents, but now we're being forced to behave as agents by the courts.

Question. When you charge people, do you set a fee in advance or do you base your fee on the purchase price?

My fees, generally speaking, are a percentage fee because it's easier, but I always disclose that there is a conflict of interest because fees rise as prices go up.

We go through a discussion and depending on the price range, we might or might not put in some way to deal with the conflict of interest. The fee differential between $100,-000 and $95,000 is something like $150 and it just isn't enough to create a real conflict of interest. A theoretical one yes, but not in practice. But if I'm dealing with $1 million property, that's a little bit different and I've dealt with that sort of thing in a number of different ways. Sometimes I work on an hourly fee, sometimes I work on a flat fee. Sometimes I work on a reduced percentage fee but put in a bonus for the differential between the sale price and the list price. The important point is you've got to disclose and discuss the fact that there is a conflict if you work on a percentage.

Question. Have you found a market for hourly consulting services?

I would say that maybe 10 to 15 percent of my practice is composed of people who come to me already knowing what property they're going to buy. They've had some initial discussions with the seller and they just come and say I want you to get this property for me. Handle it. In this circumstance, I often work on an hourly fee.

Question. What happens if the buyers have been working with a subagent?

If I am in a situation where the buyers have been working with another agent and that agent is not able to offer them buyer agency services, the buyers may come to me and say, "We've looked at the property with Jim but he can't represent us. We understand you can, would you be willing?"

The first thing I do is call Jim and say, "Mr. and Mrs. Smith have just come in, they've asked me to represent them, and we will be looking at 225 Main Street which you've already shown to them. I want you to be aware of this and if there's going to be a problem with it, I'd like to talk about it now."

Question. And when there is, what happens?
The result depends on the particular circumstances, including how much time and effort Jim has exerted. Our discussion may result in anything from paying him a sizeable "referral" fee to nothing at all.

If I pay him nothing, he may file for arbitration. However, several knowledgeable attorneys advise that a buyer agent can refuse arbitration providing the fee was paid by the seller and not by the listing broker. This is probably the subject for another book!

Question. Brokers who act as subagents often look for loyalty from buyers. Isn't what you're saying a challenge to the concept of buyer loyalty?
No. I think the only way you can assure buyer loyalty is by representing the buyer.

Question. What happens when you meet a self-seller?
Well, at least in our community, we find that most of the owners who act as for sale by owners are more than willing to pay a selling fee. They just don't want to pay the listing fee.

Question. In other words, instead of paying 6 percent they might be prepared to pay 3 percent?
Sure, and whenever I've got a buyer who's interested in a property, I ask the sellers whether they've included any kind of a selling fee. If they have, that's fine, if they haven't, then we'll have to deal with it.

Question. If the world was perfect, wouldn't it be better to be paid directly by the purchaser for buyer agency services? Why not have an offer where the seller pays a credit at closing to the buyer and the buyer can use that credit for any purpose, including a fee for buyer representation?
New Mexico is the only state we know of that has legislation

that prevents any agent from receiving a fee from anyone besides their principal. And as a result, the only way you can take a buyer agent's fee out of the transaction is to have the seller credit the buyer with an amount equivalent to whatever the buyer's agent's fee is and then have the buyer pay the buyer agent. That is really unusual though.

Question. You are near the national headquarters for RE/MAX, the largest 100-percent commission firm in the country. How does the 100-percent commission concept influence your business, or does it?
I'm an independent broker, I'm also, in today's terminology, a boutique broker. I've a very, very small brokerage house. There are four of us and prior to that I was a single agent. No agents supporting me at all. So, I'm not in competition with RE/MAX.

Question. Have you lost agents to RE/MAX or other firms?
No I haven't. What I've established is a very close group. It's almost like a family where we are supportive of each other, we assist each other, we know each other's business at least to the degree that we don't step on toes.

Question. It's often said that because of franchises and large local firms the future for small independents is bleak. Do you agree?
I think in general what they're talking about is not the small broker, but the medium-sized broker because the medium-sized broker, the guy that's got one office with 10 or 20 agents, really has to compete with the very large companies to keep his agents.

When you get down to the very small office, the one to five person office, they're not in competition with the big companies, never have been and never intend to be. They can be very profitable because you can control expenses and they tend to establish a very loyal clientele.

RICHARD J. LOUGHLIN
President and Chief Executive Officer
Century 21 Real Estate Corporation
Irvine, California

Few names in the real estate industry have greater recognition than Century 21, a worldwide franchise organization with more than 7,200 offices.

Century 21 brokers participated in approximately 705,000 real estate transactions in 1989, business that represented about one of every nine homes sold in the United States. The firm's dollar volume totaled $65 billion, while commissions distributed to the 78,000 brokers and agents in the system were valued at an estimated $2.5 billion.

Richard J. Loughlin started with Century 21 in 1973 as a regional master franchisee and developed a successful regional program in northern California. Named president and chief executive officer of the national organization in 1981, he is today recognized as one of the real estate industry's leading executives.

Question: Century 21 is now a mature, established franchise network. Where will you find future growth?

Our future growth will occur both in the United States and abroad. As a matter of fact, there are still countless opportunities for us throughout the United States. We're currently operating at a 10 or 11 percent market share and there are many large markets where we are underdeveloped.

Question: You have more than 7,000 offices. Can you have too many offices in a given area?

We use several factors to determine when we have reached a sufficient penetration standpoint.

One factor is certainly market share. If we have a number of offices in a given community that have a 20-to-30 percent market share, it is unlikely that we would want additional offices there. But with less market share, we may want to add offices.

In each of our 22 U.S. regions we are targeted to establish

one franchise for every 15,000 population, so in a community with 500,000 people we might have as many as 33 or 34 offices.

Question: Can you put too many offices in a single market?
Certainly. Any franchise could oversaturate a market and, consequently, have a negative impact on their individual franchisees. However, franchising works best when you realize sufficient penetration in each marketplace.

If we were to have one office per community, we would have no name recognition, less financial strength to provide services, and insufficient drawing power.

Question: If I have a real estate office why would I want to join Century 21?
A franchisee will come into our system because they know that a well-established brand name is a very effective marketing tool—we have an awareness factor amongst the American consuming public of around 90 percent. Nine out of ten know our name, so Century 21 is virtually synonymous with real estate. There is a tremendous advantage in having that name.

Our advertising brings more buyers and sellers to our offices. Our training programs are second to none. We have training for new sales associates, experienced associates, specialized areas of our business and management development courses for better management in our offices. I think our marketing tools, our referral system, and other factors translate into the ability to recruit quality sales associates and, consequently, more real estate transactions for our system.

Question: Are most of your franchises created from existing real estate offices or from newly-emerging businesses?
The vast majority are conversions from existing independent offices. We are happy to contract with a start-up office if we know the franchisee and we have a good feel for their capacity to manage and utilize our system.

When we sell a conversion franchise, we have the advantage of knowing what that person has accomplished in their business and the reputation they enjoy. It's just a little easier in dealing with a conversion office to decide whether or not they have the quality we want.

Question: Suppose I had an existing real estate office. How much would it cost to become a franchisee?
It would depend on a number of specifics. If you had an office with 10 or 15 sales associates in an average marketplace, you would probably be looking at a conversion cost of $25,000–$40,000. That would be the franchise fee, signs, stationery, everything you needed. However, there are some conditions where conversion could cost $100,000, so it's really hard to be specific until you know what size office you are dealing with.

Question: What makes a local office successful?
I wouldn't want to play down the advertising, training, referrals or other marketing tools, but the absolute key to success in today's and tomorrow's market is to have a large number of highly-qualified, well-trained, motivated sales associates operating from a well-managed environment.

Question: But while some sales agents are successful, its fair to say that others are not?
Far too many are not successful. It is relatively easy to secure a license and enter what appears to be a very lucrative business. However, in truth, it is a demanding and difficult career that requires knowledge and dedication. The top one-third of agents do extremely well. The middle third make an adequate income and have potential to improve. And then there's the bottom third. They're not making it, they come into the business, it sounds and looks good, but they just don't have what it takes to make it.

Question: As a franchisor, do you establish price or fee schedules for your affiliates?
No, those are established by each individual office.

Question: If an office wants to represent purchasers, is that permissible within your system?
Yes. As a matter of fact, we're seeing activity in a few market-

places where real estate offices are designing their operations to specialize in representing purchasers only and are advertising themselves as buyers' brokers.

Question: Is buyer representation now a significant factor in the marketplace?
I don't think I would refer to it as significant. It's a very small, a very minute part of the overall industry.

Question: How many states now have mandatory disclosure requirements for real estate brokers?
There are 33 states at this time that have disclosure requirements.

Question: Do you believe that brokers should be allowed to charge purchasers for mortgage information and placements?
We believe that as long as there are actual services rendered, and they are fully disclosed to the principals, it is absolutely a legitimate part of a business operation.

Question. If brokers provide mortgage information and advice, are they doing the same job that mortgage loan officers have traditionally done?
If you're giving them a variety of loans and you have access to various products that are available in the marketplace, you're virtually rendering the same service that a mortgage broker would render.

Question. Some broker-based loan information systems provide data on loans from a single company or just a few lenders. Is there a consumer issue with captive loan systems?
When you're trying to create a captive market, I think that is wrong. But if it is to be done, I believe total disclosure must be made to the buyers. You should make it very clear that you are recommending this loan because you have an affiliation with this one loan company and that the buyer certainly has the right to secure other information or to seek other sources.

Question: Who owns Century 21?
We're owned by Metropolitan Life.

Question: If I'm a real estate broker can I also sell insurance?
Some of our franchisees are licensed as insurance agents and
they disclose to buyers that they have the capability of plac-
ing insurance on that property. If there is an insurance commission to them it is fully disclosed.

*Question: If I'm both an insurance agent and a Century 21
broker, can I sell insurance from someone other than Metropolitan Life?*
Our franchisees can deal with any insurance company they
want. We have many franchisees who have had insurance
operations long before Metropolitan Life acquired us, and
many continue to do business with other insurance firms.

*Question: Does Century 21 provide health or pension benefits
for agents and brokers?*
There are very few pension programs being administered in
our industry and as a franchising organization, we have not
become involved in health insurance for our system because
the marketplace has pretty well taken care of these needs.

*Question: Has the emergence of 100-percent brokers had much
influence on your operations?*
No, the 100-percent broker has had little impact on us. However, that concept is a competitive force in the marketplace
and their share of market is growing, but it has not had a
significant impact on our operations.
   The 100-percent broker concept is a misnomer. The sales
associate in this type of operation pays a large monthly desk
rental fee and other additional expenses and then retains all
of the commission. In actuality, the net result could be far less
to this sales associate than they would receive through a
traditional commission split with their broker.

Question: If not from you, who is losing market share?
Probably the smaller independents who are having a more
and more difficult time surviving.

Question: What about small brokers? Will they be squeezed out?

The mom and pop broker will continue to exist but I think there are going to be fewer and fewer of them.

To succeed, the mom and pop brokers will have to maintain a very high profile in their community, they'll need outstanding sales people, a strong geographic and demographic niche in their particular marketplace and they're going to have to be good managers.

Question: Will regional giants remain competitive?

I don't think they're really threatened, but in addition to good management, they're going to need a national referral system to bring them buyers from outside their local marketplace.

Question: Will referral networks convert to franchise status?

Many of the referral services are now starting to look at franchising and I think that's a trend you may see over the next few years.

Question: Are there too many licensees nationwide?

I think there have been more licenses granted than our industry really needs, but fortunately they're not all active in the business.

Question: Should we have tougher qualifications for brokers and agents?

I don't think there's a correlation between classroom hours and consumer satisfaction or quality of service. Personally, I think you need a sufficient number of hours in that classroom so you can become familiar with all of the necessary forms, contracts, etc., know what your legal obligations are, and what conduct the industry expects from a licensee.

Question: If not in the classroom, where are agents learning the brokerage business?

They're learning to be successful through training through their system or within their offices, and that's part of what we offer.

Question: Why should a broker with six months' experience charge the same fee as the 20-year veteran?

It's not longevity necessarily that gives a consumer the best service. I think that the offices that are successful, that run high volume, can ask more for their services than an office which has been around for a number of years but is unable to bring more buyers and sellers together.

I don't think there's any correlation between being in business for 20 years and being in business for one year. You take an office that's only been in business for one year that is well managed, has attracted high-quality sales associates, has a big advertising program, a referral network and many times they can do a lot more for a client than an office that's been in business 20 years.

Question: Can it make sense to have a single office with several commission systems?

Yes it will work. Many of our offices, and many offices within the industry, do that. It's difficult sometimes to manage, but it does work.

Many of our offices have different commission splits predicated on the agent's volume.

Question: Where is the real estate business heading?

We're going to see a far more professional, higher quality real estate service. We're going to see a continued growth in nationwide and regional brokerage firms and franchises. I think this will be at the expense of some of the smaller firms and weaker managed regional operations.

The subagency situation has been looked at by government agencies for 10 to 15 years and changes there have been very moderate. Most change has been in the disclosure area only and so it hasn't been very impactful.

In mortgage financing there will be major changes over the next decade, driven by competition—new types of mortgages, new sources of financing, emerging convertible mortgages, no closing points or up front fees, inflation-indexed mortgages, that type of thing.

The MLS system will be under a continual scrutiny from the Justice Department and other government agencies, but I don't think much will happen. There's a lot of government bureaucrats that are somewhat naive in their zeal to try to reform a system that really works very well the way it is.

DAVID LINIGER
Chief Executive Officer
RE/MAX International, Inc.
Englewood, Colorado

Few people have caused more change in the real estate industry than Dave Liniger, co-founder and chief executive officer of RE/MAX International, the firm most responsible for raising agent incomes nationwide.

Agents typically split commissions with brokers on a 50/50 basis until RE/MAX popularized the 100-percent commission system. With a 100-percent plan there is no commission split—agents keep every dollar they earn while brokers receive a monthly fee from each agent. To compete with RE/MAX, other brokers have been forced to offer higher commission splits to top producers, splits that have radically changed traditional industry economics.

Convinced and direct, Liniger has built a franchise chain that is the largest real estate operation in Canada and vying for the top position in the United States. In 1989, the company completed more than 700,000 transactions.

Question: Did you encounter much opposition when you first began RE/MAX?
That would be an understatement. Certain brokers tried to blackball us from local real estate groups, they tried to deny us access to the multiple listing services. The disinformation campaign was unbelievable.

At one point, RE/MAX was under investigation by the FBI for fraudulently selling houses with VA and FHA loans. We were under investigation by the Securities and Exchange Commission (SEC) for illegally offering securities even though we had never sold stock in our lives. We were under investigation by state real estate commissions who came in and audited our trust accounts weekly because they kept getting anonymous tips and letters and postcards saying RE/MAX was spending buyer funds. People went to the state attorney general's office and said we were violating fair trade practices. Basically, there was a tremendous attempt to drive us out of business.

In every single audit we were never off a penny, everything was exactly letter-perfect. The SEC said, hey, we'd never sold anything. The FBI said you guys haven't done anything wrong.

Question: Did you sue for restraint of trade?
At the time we did not because we didn't have any money. In the past 5 or 10 years, we've had to have our attorneys talk to various people and explain the penalties for anti-trust activities. In every single case, those activities have ceased.

Question: Are you now more accepted within the industry?
Very much so. When you're the new kid on the block you're extremely controversial. Now RE/MAX is an accepted entity, and many of our people are leaders on their boards. We're no longer controversial.

Question: How has RE/MAX given agents marketplace leverage?
Over the years I've been introduced at various conventions as the single individual who has given more pay raises to more real estate agents than anybody else in the history of our industry.

Because we are paying attention to the top producer, the rest of the industry has had to come as close as they can to matching our compensation programs and that has forced up payments to top agents.

Question: Why should a top producer join RE/MAX when he or she can start his own firm?
Think about how inefficient our industry has been when 20 people want to go out and open 20 independently owned and operated companies, each one a mom and pop company. Each one of those 20 little offices has to have 2 or 3 telephone lines, even though there's only one person working because you can't have a busy signal when you're trying to get listings or sales. Each has to have a separate copy machine, a FAX machine, a computer, and a conference room and so many separate facilities are very, very inefficient.

Cooperatives work with attorneys and cooperatives have worked with architects and doctors, so why not in real estate?

That is why 20 people only need 15 or 16 telephone lines—they don't need two apiece because most real estate agents are out of the office working at any one time, so there is plenty of excess. They can have one large copy machine—that's much cheaper divided by 20 people than having one small copy machine apiece. They can have group advertising. They can go on vacations because there's somebody to run their business.

Question: What monthly fees can I expect to pay as an agent?
Each office is independently owned and operated. We do not dictate fee structure. We dictate the concept which is that every sales associate is expected to participate in the cost of running an office.

Agents have three basic costs:

The first is a fee for office management.

The second cost is the equally-shared expense of running an office. If you have 15 sales associates in an office, they will divide to the penny whatever costs can be shared on an equal basis; janitorial service, the electric bill, the telephone bill except for long distance calls, the secretary's salary, the copy machine or whatever it might be.

And the third expense category is what each sales associate spends individually for promotion, multiple listing fees, brochures, dues, business cards, etc.

Question: The items in that third category are passed through at cost or on a cost-plus basis?
On a cost basis. In many markets, because we are the largest single real estate advertiser, we can get the largest discounts and pass them through to agents. A lot of times our people are paying half the cost for advertising than they would otherwise pay if they opened a small independent office.

Question: Although you do not dictate monthly fees, what costs might an agent encounter?
It varies dramatically, but it would average somewhere between $1,200 to $1,400 a month. The differences are caused by the size of the office, the market share that the real estate organization has in a particular area, and the type of office.

Some of our offices are very successful. They've been open

10–12 years. The agents are very, very, financially successful and they don't mind paying a $1,500 or $1,800 expense in return for a plush private office and other facilities.

Question: Around the country some markets have seen declining sales. What has happened to your affiliates in areas where sales have slowed?
If you look at the areas of the country that have been hardest hit, the RE/MAX organization in each of those areas has increased market share and agent income has increased.

Question: Even in declining markets?
You bet. Let me explain why. In a traditional real estate company you have a mix of sales associates who are very experienced and a lot more who are slightly experienced and moderately productive. You also have a tremendous number of beginners and part-timers that come in and never make it.

When a market turns down, the first people to get hurt are the beginners, part-timers and low-producers. They get hurt the most because they're the most inexperienced and they're trying to learn the industry—learn license law, learn real estate law, and also find customers at the same time.

Now if you look at a top producer who has been around 10 or 12 years, they've been in a bad market or two. Whether they're ours or they work with another company, they are getting about 70 or 80 percent of their business from referrals and repeat customers. They've worked with 10, 15, 20 buyers a year for the last 10 years and they have a pool of prospects, including many who are active even in a down market.

Top producers are top producers not because they're super sales people, they're top producers because they give darned good service and somebody says, yeah, I'm going to use them again. When a market turns bad, top producers don't have time to knock on doors or go around the neighborhoods trying to find business. They're getting business by word-of-mouth and through past contacts.

Question: Do you have offices outside urban and suburban areas?

Sure. Our emphasis has always been selling in metropolitan areas because it's much easier to sell 50 franchises within a 45-minute driving radius then to go to a rural area 200 miles away to find an interested broker. We do have offices in small areas that have three and four sale associates.

Question: In early 1990, RE/MAX had 1,673 offices and 27,506 agents. How much more growth do you expect?

We believe in the 80/20 rule; that is, 20 percent of the agents make 80 percent of the sales. And what we've said is that we'd like to have half of that top 20 percent, which is 10 percent, and to capture 30 to 35 percent of all sales.

Question: RE/MAX has grown tremendously in the past decade. As businesses mature their rate of growth declines. Are you reaching a point where your business has matured?

No. We're just getting started. Right now in the United States we have almost 20,000 sales associates, about 8,000 in Canada. The Canadians have room for another 1,000 sales associates. In the United States, with our 19,500 or 20,000 agents, we feel we're one-fourth of the way. We have tremendous room for growth.

Question: How has the concept of a real estate office changed since you first started?

When we opened in 1973 our early offices were approximately 1,200 square feet. We originally opened our offices thinking we ought to have about 10 to 12 people and that most of them would not have private offices, just a bullpen just like our competition at the time.

We would have file cabinets, metal furniture with nice enamel colors, one computer hooked into the multiple listing service, and one secretary. It was easy to open an office for let's say $10,000–$15,000 in cash plus notes and leases and that sort of thing for another $20,000 to $30,000.

Now what's happened with the RE/MAX organization is that inflation has set in. The cost of office space has risen—in Denver it's gone from $6 per square foot to $12 to $15. Also, we've upgraded our facilities so that many of our agents have private offices. We've gone to beautiful furniture. We've gone to two and three computers at $30,000 or $40,000, FAX machines, our own phone systems and so on.

And so the difference was that when we first started in 1973, we realistically could open an office for $20,000 cash and say $50,000 in notes. Today to open a RE/MAX office generally takes in the neighborhood of $50,000 to $75,000 cash and $250,000 or more in additional lines of credit and notes.

It's not the same. We don't do 10 and 12 person offices anymore. Our average office—one that's been open more than two years—has 28 sales associates.

Question: In addition to $50,000 to $70,000 in cash I would need to open a RE/MAX franchise, what other costs would I face?
There is a franchise fee. It varies from $15,000 to $20,000 approximately.

Question: And you would have an override also on the gross income for the office?
Yes, from each one of the sales associates.

Question: So essentially, you are a franchise in the same sense as McDonald's or whatever?
Yes.

Question: Is getting a franchise just a matter of money?
In some of our most successful regions such as a Colorado, California, northern Illinois, we probably turn down nine out of every ten people who come in. Half were probably turned down because they may not have had sufficient liquidity to carry the office.

Question: How long does it take to reach a break-even status in the typical case?
Our successful broker/owners recruit in the neighborhood of one to two sales associates a month over and above any agents they start with. If they set up a 15 person office, they probably will not be breaking even until sometime after 6 to 9 months.

We've had an office open in Denver a year and a half ago, and they went from zero agents to 30 agents in less than 2 months. But that is very, very unique. There probably isn't one in 50 that ever accomplishes that. Most of them were just like us. They open, they start recruiting. At the end of month one they get a couple agents, after month two they get four agents.

We try to tell them, don't start a 40-person office. Don't start a 35-person office. Start a 15–20-person office. You'll get to break-even within 6 months to a year and until then you'll have to pay the negative cash flow from your commissions or other assets. After you're up and three years into your lease, then look at doubling the space and adding another 15 agents.

Question: Not all of your franchises are successful, correct?
No, they are not.

Question: Are RE/MAX agents independent contractors?
Yes.

Question: If I'm a RE/MAX agent, can I offer my services on a discount basis?
Yes.

Question: If I'm a RE/MAX agent, can I act as a buyer broker?
That's okay.

Question: That's not an issue for you?
You have to understand something. The law of the land is that you can't be involved in price fixing and you can't dictate certain business practices.

Not only do we very sincerely say it's the law of the land but we also observe what the spirit of the law is and there's nothing wrong with competing on price. Incidentally, that does not make us popular with the rest of the business.

Question: Can a RE/MAX agent obtain compensation from a lender for providing mortgage information or mortgage services?
The policy of the company is that they may not do so.

Question: Is it alright if a purchaser voluntarily makes a payment for loan services or information?
I do not believe it would be alright. What you have to understand is that we're in the real estate business, not the mortgage business.

Just like everybody else, we're very interested in being able to offer mortgages on site. Everybody has attempted to do that. We probably have eight or ten of our brokers somewhere in the system with their own mortgage operation but we monitor them very closely and say they can't compensate agents for bringing in loan business.

If the law changed and allowed referral fees, we would change our policy as long as the customer knew that the agent was being paid a fee for providing a loan service. Full written disclosure would be an absolute must if they changed the law.

Question: But even if there was full disclosure, is there a potential for conflict between the role of getting the mortgage and selling the property?
Of course. In our industry there's tremendous room for conflict on everything that we do.

Question: Many states now require agency disclosure statements. How have such statements influenced your business?
I think a disclosure statement protects everybody in the transaction—buyer, seller, real estate broker and real estate agent. If you have all of the aspects of a transaction in writing, then you have little chance for litigation.

If a sales associate wants to buy a house, for instance, then he or she needs to state in the offer that they have a real estate license and may earn a fee.

Question: Normally profits for a real estate firm are related to sales and listings. In a RE/MAX office they are related more directly, not totally, to the issue of how well the franchisee can recruit top agents. In other words, isn't the franchisee's goal somewhat different than a traditional broker?
Suppose we have a shopping center. The shopping center has the ability to lease space on the basis of $12 a square foot or a combined rate of $5 per foot plus 2 percent of gross sales.

Every landlord wants 100-percent occupancy with as few vacancies as possible. The ultimate goal of the person who charges a fee per square foot is no different from the goal of the person who charges by gross sales.

Question: Generally agents in your system receive 100 percent of the commissions they generate, but 100-percent payments are banned in several states. Why?

We asked several real estate commissions about that. We wanted to know if we could have a 50/50 commission split with our agents, and they said, "50/50 is okay, we can't dictate your commission split."

So then we asked about an 80/20 split, a split that is widely advertised. Is that legal? "Well of course that's legal."

What about 95/5? "Of course," they said, "that's legal, we can't dictate commission splits to you."

Great. We'll be on 95/5.

Question: But you still can't have 100-percent splits in some states?

I think you'll see that change in the near future. I mean listen to the logic of it.

Question: Can flat-fee and discount brokers hurt your business?

No, I don't think so, but only a fool sits and says that changes will never affect me. We sit and brainstorm and think and meet with our brokers constantly about changes in the industry. Discount brokerage firms have a place, no question about it, just as much as Charles Schwab was able to do something different for the securities industry.

We said, we can't be all things to all people and so we are going to specialize in the nation's top producing sales associates. Most of those top producing sales associates are getting the majority of their business from referrals and repeat customers and because they're top producers, very good sales people, they themselves shun working as discount brokers.

Discount brokerage firms are competing to get business on price, we're trying to build our empire with the very best sales people who are best at giving service and who will appeal to our market niche. I think there's room for both concepts, but I'm personally skeptical about discounting because there's far more to selling a house than putting a listing in the MLS book and putting out a sign that says for sale by owner.

Question: What about small independent brokers, is there a niche for them too?
You bet there is. They have a perfect niche because the very small independent broker has total and complete control over expenses. If they work out of their house, if they have a small office, if they have almost no secretarial service and so on, they have very, very low overhead and so they don't have to make many sales to generate $25,000 or $30,000 or $40,000 a year.

I think the small broker is always going to be there but the question is will that small broker make more money if they become part of a big cooperative and have better name recognition that brings additional business.

Question: As a franchisee, I'm a broker and I'm responsible for the agents and the associate brokers in my office. Have you had supervision problems?
No. Some traditional brokers have tried to say that RE/MAX is just a rent-a-desk operation but the truth is that in an era of litigation you have to be darned sure of what your agents are doing.

We have sales meetings. We have training sessions, we have audio-visual aids, we have cassette training programs, we have quarterly sales meetings, we have some of the best experts in law and everything else that's out there. We do everything any other brokerage does. We have floor time and we tour our listings.

We counsel our agents. If an agent gets to the point where they're not making any sales, his bill continues. If we look at the agent and he's not making sales, we're counseling with the agent saying, how are you going to pay your bill next month if you don't have anything under contract this month?

Question: You emphasize that your agents are productive. Do they stand out for any other reason?

We have three times as many CRSs (Certified Residential Specialists) per capita in our operation as the rest of the industry. We have more CRBs (Certified Residential Brokers) per capita and CCIMs (Certified Commercial Investment Members) per capita than the rest of the industry.

Question: Have you seen more attorneys entering the real estate business?

No, not at all. I suppose some get a real estate license so they can broker their own deals.

I like attorneys. Everyone maligns them, for the most part, but the vast majority are doing things from estate planning to tax planning to helping. Attorneys are not nearly the problem to our industry that everybody makes them out to be.

Question: Can I set up a 100-percent firm to compete with RE/MAX?

A lot of people have tried. In 1978 we were tracking 937 competing 100-percent companies.

We had achieved some notoriety in Denver and I went on the seminar circuit to a couple of hundred cities. We were mailing out brochures and tales of our success in Denver spread throughout the country.

An awful lot of people looked at our materials and threw them away. Of the people who kept it and were interested, there were a tremendous number who said, well, what do I need them for, why don't I just get their forms and I'll imitate their system and we'll be a smashing overnight success.

The problem that everybody did not understand is that there were successful 100-percent companies before RE/MAX. A company in Phoenix had made it work before we did, and there was a company in Calgary, Canada that had made it work before they did.

The problem is it's not just a one office network. We took the concept of a very professional and successful firm with private offices, secretarial help, massive advertising programs, and all things that made it so good and married that concept to the 100-percent commission to have the best of two worlds.

What's happening now is a lot of people are saying we

have succeeded because of the 100-percent concept. It isn't
the commission alone, it's the 100-percent concept combined with all the other things that bring additional business
to the agency.

*Question: Suppose a company had agents with a traditional
commission split and some paid on 100-percent basis operating
from the same office. Could that work?*
It's been tried dozens and dozens of times. And every person
I've seen try it so far has eventually gone out of business.

JAMES J. HALL
Broker-Owner
James J. Hall, Inc., Realtors
Silver Spring, Maryland

While much attention is given to large real estate firms and national franchises, independent brokers are active in every community. Figures from the National Association of Realtors show that small firms, those with 10 or fewer agents, represent one-third of the real estate workforce. Small firms also enjoy higher sales per full-time associate and generate proportionately greater pre-tax earnings than large competitors.

Jim Hall graduated from the University of Florida, served in the Army, and then entered the real estate business in 1963. He has served for more than a decade as a director of the Maryland Association of Realtors, was twice elected president of the Maryland, Delaware and District of Columbia chapter of RESSI (the Real Estate Securities and Syndication Institute), and was the first president of the Maryland Real Estate Educators Association.

Hall operates from a single office and has fewer than 10 agents, the classic description of a small broker. He offers a broad array of services, however, including sales, management and syndication for investors.

In this era of full disclosure, readers should know that Jim Hall is a friend and business associate, someone I have known for many years.

Question. Just how small is small?
Very small. Basically, we have a few agents, my wife does property management, and I do sales.

Question. You're not on television and you don't place full-page ads in the local paper. How do you get business?
Anyone who has been in the real estate business for several years should have built up a reasonable number of centers of influence such as former clients and customers. By staying in contact with them and developing new prospects you should be able to maintain a successful business. It's just that simple.

Question. So today's income is based on past performance?
Without income generated from referrals it would be tough
to stay in business. A good customer/client follow-up system
is a must.

*Question. How do you analyze your company dollar as com-
pared to how a large company would look at income?*
In looking at the company dollar there is very little, if any,
difference between the large firm and the small firm. Both
must scrutinize income and expenses, the cost attributed to
each individual agent as compared to productivity, and the
climate of the market place at any given time. Depending on
the kind of market you're in, you may want to increase or cut
down on expenses such as newspaper advertising and mail-
ings.

*Question. You buy and sell properties for investors. Do you
invest yourself and if so, how do you structure such deals?*
Many times when I put together a group of investors to
purchase a property I am asked if I am going to invest also.
If my answer is "no" it's hard to explain.

When we did our first limited partnership it was designed
as an investment opportunity for our agents and I acted as
the general partner so I had to invest in those transactions.

As far as the structure, if we have a large number of investors we will probably do a limited partnership. These are not
public offerings. Some of the basic guidelines we established
early on were: all the properties must be in the state of
Maryland where we operate, the investors must be citizens
of Maryland, we do not advertise for investors, we only invite
people we know to invest, and the investors must meet our
qualification standards.

If it is a small deal or we only have a few investors, we may
take title as tenants in common with other owners. There is
always an agreement that details many issues, including what
percentage of ownership is needed to sell or mortgage the
property.

Question. Are there advantages in dealing with investors?
Investment properties create several kinds of income. First,

you have a sales commission when your investor acquires the property. Second you have the property management and leasing fees during the holding period. And third, you have the listing and sales commissions when it is time for the investor to sell or trade.

As for when, it depends on the market conditions at any given time. Investors will call and say, gee, I have a little bit of money I'd like to invest, how about now?

If it's a good market, like we had during most of the mid and late 1980s, it's a seller's market. Now, with a real slow-down in residential market, a glut of office space, the banking industry problems, and other factors, I am starting to call my investors and tell them it is time to buy.

Question. You once operated several offices with many agents. Were there drawbacks to running a larger firm?
There were several reasons I decided to get away from a situation with lots of salespeople.

I got tired of working seven days and seven nights a week. When you've got 50 salespeople and they know your home phone number, you can't hide.

Plus, we have four kids and I wanted to spend more time with them and my wife.

Question. Are required educational standards tough enough for today's market?
No, standards are way too low. The number of classroom hours required for licensing should be greatly increased and standards for real estate instructors should be raised. The number of required continuing education hours should also be increased with a greater emphasis on keeping up with new real estate laws and regulations.

Question. Many of your transactions are long-term deals. How do you generate the income you need between big sales?
Not every deal is long-term. If you're dealing with improved property—residential, commercial, or industrial—those are immediate turnovers.

The only time you're looking at a long-range project is with land, so you want other projects to balance out your income. You work on the small stuff along with the large deals that include syndication, joint ventures, selling small commercial properties.

Question. Have agency disclosure laws hurt your activities as a broker?
No, it's something we should have had all along. Our clients and customers love disclosure.

Question. Do you care if an agent is paid on a traditional basis, on a discount, or with a 100-percent fee?
It doesn't make any difference how a co-op agent is paid, it's none of my business. When I meet a co-op agent for the first time, hopefully their business card will show a designation, whether they are a GRI (a graduate of the Realtors Institute), or CRS (a Certified Residential Specialist), or CRB (a Certified Residential Broker). I just want to work with somebody who knows what they're doing.

Question. Is there room for flat-fee and discount brokers?
There's room for everybody. Services can vary, fees can vary. I don't see anything wrong with people listing for any commission or any fee schedule as long as the client understands what services will be provided, and—just as importantly— what services will not be provided.

Question. Are big companies your main competitors?
In real estate you are competing more with individual agents than with the size of the company. Some sellers will list with large firms just because they are large. Basically what I tell sellers is that it does not matter how large the company is if you don't have a good agent.

Question. How has the MLS evolved?
It went from books and 3 × 5 listing cards to dumb terminals to PCs. I think it's fantastic. You can give better service, you're better informed, and the technology is still progressing very, very fast.

Question. Suppose subagency was outlawed tomorrow. How would it influence your business?
Without subagency the only other alternative would be the

growth of buyer broker activity. If subagency ended I would run an ad in the newspaper saying we want buyer brokers to show our listings.

Question. Are there too many agents and brokers?
Yes, in the sense that there are too many licensees who don't keep up with the current laws, regulations, and trends. They don't know what's going on in their communities as far as zoning, planning, highways, all those things.

That's the only reason there are too many agents. The number doesn't matter, it's quality.

Question. Why should a new agent expect to earn the same fees as someone who has been in business 20 years?
If a new agent can do the same job as the one with 20 years experience the pay should be the same. The same could be said of a gold or oil prospector, a football player, or a surgeon. It's the productivity that counts.

Question. Why do you have a property management business?
Property management works hand in glove with everything else we do. It's an income supplement. In our case, maybe about 30 percent of the gross.

Anytime you have property management it means you have an investor/owner. If you have an investor/owner, that investor/owner can do one of three things: buy more investment property, trade for other investment property, or sell investment property. So you're creating sales and you're creating listings. When you look at each facet of your business, it all ties together.

Question. Being small, how do you manage properties if you're out of town?
My wife, Mary, handles property management totally. I don't get involved in it. She handles both commercial and residential property. When we are out of town there is always the telephone. Our service can reach us at any time and Mary has developed a really good group of contractors and service people to take care of any emergency that may arise. If she has a property being offered for lease while we are out of

town she will ask another property manager to handle the leasing for her. Mary has chaired the real estate industry's local Property Management Committee and been active for many years with other brokers who offer property management services, so it's easy for her to get help from other managers when needed.

Question. How can large firms engage in buyer representation?
All the large companies should have their own entity for buyer brokerage that is separate from their seller representation. The need is there. Every buyer needs to have the advice of a good real estate agent.

Question. How do you use buyer representation in your practice?
I have clients, including some of the larger developers in the area. They say, "Jim, we want property in a certain location." They identify the property and ask me to buy it for them. They give me complete instructions as to price, terms and conditions.

I write the contract, do the negotiating within the guidelines my client has given me and then assign the contract to my client when we have a firm deal. The seller understands that I represent a purchaser and that I will assign the contract; there is total disclosure. That's one way of doing it.

Another way is to identify a property not on the market, one that has zoning, location, utilities; a property that has no problems with adequate public facilities yet meets the development requirements of one of my builders. I will go to that builder with all my information and ask if there is any interest. If there is we sign a buyer broker agreement and I try to acquire the property for the builder.

Then I can go to a landowner and say you don't have to pay me any commission, the buyer is paying my fee. We'd like to buy the property, here's the offer.

Question. What if you identify a property for a builder and they buy it without you?
They're not in business very long if they do that. I think almost every builder or developer bends over backwards to

protect brokers who bring them properties. Usually, if you take a builder a piece of property, he's tickled to death, he loves to pay you, really.

The thing about selling land is that if you call the largest builder in the metropolitan area and leave a message, "I have this piece of land I would like to tell you about," that builder will call you back.

Question. Is it true you're in the moving business?
One of my buyer/clients is putting properties together for development. There's a nice old house on the land and I asked what he was going to do with the house, and he said, "we're going to bulldoze it."

And I said, would you give it to me if I move it. He said yes, so I have a seven-bedroom, three-story house for just the lot cost and moving expense.

Question. What is the moving cost?
It'll cost $18,000 to move. So if you figure you're going to buy a lot and it needs some work, that's okay. It's going to cost me a total of about $100,000 for moving, site work and the lot. That's not bad for a seven-bedroom, three-story house in a nice section of eastern Montgomery County.

Question. Isn't it difficult to move a house?
You can hardly move a three-story house on the street. It's really involved. You have to coordinate with the state police, the county police, the electric company, the telephone company and almost everybody else.

Moving a rambler is easy, moving an old three-story house is tough. But in this case there is a lot within 400 feet of the present location, so the house doesn't have to travel very far.

P. WESLEY FOSTER
President
Long & Foster, Realtors
Fairfax, Virginia

In 1968 Wes Foster and Henry Long started their real estate business in a small Virginia office just outside Washington, DC. Fueled by government expansion, a continuing population influx, and massive private-sector development, the capital area emerged as one of the best real estate markets in the country. And as the capital region expanded, the young real estate firm also grew and prospered.

By 1989 Long & Foster had 175 offices and was selling 40,000 properties a year—by unit volume the largest independent real estate firm in the United States. Sales in 1989 totaled $6.4 billion and Long & Foster offices could be found from Baltimore to Norfolk.

From a spacious Virginia office with handsome furnishings and notable sculpture by his wife, Wes Foster presides over a business that today includes more than 5,400 agents. His firm is a model within the real estate industry—a company that started small, grew continuously for more than 20 years, and now seeks still further growth and expansion.

Question: Is it true that one of your earliest offices was in a Holiday Inn?

Yes. When we had three offices in Virginia, a retired Air Force officer came to us and said he wanted to open an office for us in Manassas (Virginia, site of the famous Civil War battle). He looked around and what he came back with was the Holiday Inn.

We thought that would be a good place to start until we could find a permanent office, so we opened in the Holiday Inn and found out pretty soon that many IBM transferees moving into the area stayed there.

After they'd had breakfast or dinner, the transferees walked the halls, they would happen to see us, and they were in the market for a house. Business was so good we kept that office even when we opened a bigger one down the street.

In 1974 when we decided to expand out of Virginia and into Maryland, we wanted to start in Bethesda but everybody had been there so long that we were afraid the established old-timers would beat us to death before we could get started.

So we looked further out and thought well, if we go to Gaithersburg everybody up there is so new they won't know how new we are and maybe we can get a toe-hold in that market. And the other thing that we noticed when we went up to Gaithersburg was that there was a Holiday Inn with an IBM plant across the street and we thought, well, we'll do it again.

We asked them to build us space like we had in Manassas but they wouldn't do it, we were too new and young and underfinanced. We were still fairly determined, so we picked out the room closest to the lobby and being tough real estate negotiators, negotiated the rate down to $30 a day for a 30-day month. This was negotiated from a daily rate of $31.64 at the time.

We paid them $900 a month for that room, took the beds out, put six desks in, and used the bathroom for storage because we could use the bathroom down the hall.

That is a true story and we are still in that Holiday Inn, though now in a regular office facility. We also have 6,000 square feet in our main Gaithersburg office just down the street and today we totally dominate that area.

Question: Suppose Smith wants to work with Long & Foster. What should Smith expect in terms of training in the first year?
We have a Long & Foster Institute of Real Estate. What we're doing there is not teaching how to sell real estate but how to pass the real estate exam. It's fairly technical and we have, I think, the highest pass ratio of any school in Virginia, Maryland, or DC.

Then when you have finished with the basic licensure class, we have a "Fast Start" course, a nitty-gritty, 60-hour course which explains how to really get out and list and sell real estate.

After that, a new agent goes into one of our branch offices and our branch manager sets aside two or three hours a week to sit down with new agents and provide hands-on training until they're ready to fly.

Question: With such training, what can new agents expect to earn in their first year?

A reasonable prospect, I would say, is $20,000 to $30,000 for the first year but honestly, some very good agents don't do that well the first year, they're slow starting. There's some that don't make even $20,000 that first year and they turn out to be very good agents. And there's some that take off like a rocket and make $40,000 to $60,000 that first year and occasionally even more, but that's unusual.

Question: It is commonly stated that 20 percent of all agents leave the real estate business each year. How much turnover among current agents does Long & Foster experience?

About the same. A lot of people hear that this is a wonderful business, they hear about the people who make $500,000 a year, though they're few and far between. But there are a lot of people who aren't cut out for this business. You can't be sure how successful they're going to be until you put them to the test, so we take in people thinking they're going to be a success, but they just aren't. They get out of the business.

Question: How do part-time agents fit into your system?

We take some agents that have other jobs. We don't consider them usually part-time. We like not to call them part-timers but instead people who have other employment.

We take only the ones who are effective or we ask them to go with somebody else. But let me tell you case in point: The top agent in our company sold $40 million worth of property last year. Before he came with us, he was a Light Colonel in the Air Force, gave them a full 40 hours a week but he also sold about $7–$8 million worth of real estate in his last year with the Air Force. Well, we love that kind of agent with other employment and we have a fair number of those people.

Question: Why would a successful broker continue to work with you. Why not emulate Wes Foster and go out and start an independent firm?

Well, there are certainly some people who leave us and do start their own offices. I would think that many agents don't want the responsibility of paying the rent and doing all of the other things you have to do to start an office. Also we pay well and give much in the way of support services.

We pay our top agent on a very high year-round commission schedule. We pay his postage and he is a heavy mailer. We give him secretarial support, management support and free rent. He has a pretty good deal and I think he knows that. He doesn't quite want to take that next step, we hope, and go in business for himself.

Question: One strategy you have used to expand is to buy other companies. How do you buy a real estate firm, companies that tend to have few assets?
We have a way to do it that seems to work for us, it seems to be fairly fail-safe.

The way we have bought every company is we never buy the entire company. We collapse the corporation and then we don't have any of the problems that might otherwise be there. We buy the assets, not liabilities, and pay the owner a high percent of the company dollar for the sales on the books that have not settled and a lesser percent for unsold listings. If we keep the office, we pay for the furniture and fixtures. We also pay a small percent of the agents' income, usually for two to three years.

The formula changes according to the market and the firm. We'll go in and say, "Mr. Owner—or Ms. Owner—you want to sell your firm and if you have a figure in mind perhaps we can make a deal because, basically, what we're buying are the agents. If the agents don't come with us, we don't pay anything." If they have a reasonable figure, if they truly want to sell, we can get together.

Question: If an an agent is highly-successful why split fees with Long & Foster. Why not join a 100-percent commission broker?
They have become a challenge, but right now the market is slow so we don't feel they're that much of a challenge. We're getting more agents back from 100-percent companies at this time than we are losing. We're still losing one or two but

I also don't think the challenge will go away. One-hundred percent brokers—as a group—have become the largest factor in the Atlanta, Dallas, Denver, Chicago, and Toronto markets.

Question: To combat 100-percent firms, would you consider creating offices where some agents have a conventional commission arrangement and others are on the 100-percent system? In that way you would always have cash coming in to cover overhead and operating expenses.
There are several companies around the country doing exactly that, and it is in the realm of possibility.

Question: Is it true that 20 percent of all agents capture 80 percent of all the business?
It's not totally true, but I would say that the top 20, 30, 40 percent of our agents do a great portion of our business. I don't think our top 20 percent do 80 percent of our business, no.

We have a nice core of middle income agents that we really care about and interestingly enough, we have lost more of those $60,000 to $80,000 agents to the 100-percent firms than our very top agents.

Question: To keep productive agents, brokers are offering bigger and bigger commission percentages to top producers. Have we reached a point where it is no longer profitable for the broker to employ top agents?
That's true, but we want them anyway.

Question: Why?
For market penetration. If you have market penetration, it feeds on itself. Top agents attract other agents that you do make a little money on.

Question: Given that your firm and other large brokers often list and sell a majority of the homes in a particular market, why do you belong to an MLS? By belonging to an MLS you are effectively subsidizing small competitors by giving them access to your listings.

Well, I guess we've been so busy with our thing we haven't thought about it a lot. Belonging to an MLS gets our inventory out there, gets it sold fast.

Question: Why not start your own in-house MLS? You have enough business internally and you could then reduce co-op fees to other brokers?
I think for our seller's sake we want to get homes sold just as quickly as we can. We love to sell as many as we can in-house, but we love to have the other people selling them too. The thought of starting our own MLS hasn't been high on our list.

Question: An NAR study shows that as firms become larger, profits per sale decline. Would Long & Foster be more profitable if it were smaller?
Not really. Nearly every year we make a little less on every deal, but we also make more deals. In effect, especially in the good years, we do very well.

We're also a very financially prudent company, so as we face this down-turn, we face it with no debt and with a lot of money in the bank. That's a nice way to face a soft market.

Question: When individuals work for a corporation they often obtain such benefits as health insurance, profit sharing, and pensions. Since real estate agents are independent contractors, how do they obtain such benefits?
Let's start with health insurance. We do have a group plan which agents can buy that is very competitive. Many of our agents have insurance through their spouses or because of past military or federal service.

On their retirement, they have IRAs and then if they are astute—and many of them are very astute—they do what all good real estate agents should do over the years, and that's buy property. I can't think of any better retirement vehicle than good real estate.

Question: Would Long & Foster have been so successful if you were located in a depressed market?
Probably not. We've got to give a lot of credit to the local market because if you're in a slow metropolitan area or a

small town, you can only do what's possible. We have one of the most dynamic markets—they're beginning to call the Washington/Baltimore/Norfolk corridor the golden crescent.

Washington/Baltimore now has 6 million people and will probably grow to 8 million in the coming decade, and Norfolk is pretty dynamic itself. So, an awful lot of opportunity is in this region, it's an interesting point.

Question: Can one of your brokers or agents act as a buyer broker?
We do some buyer brokerage presently, but we don't show our own listings because of dual agency concerns. There are other firms that act as buyer brokers and show our listings, but we've not seen a great deal of it.

Question: Will you pass through a portion of your commission to a buyer's agent?
We may negotiate a deal so that the buyers are happy with what they're paying for the house, but the buyer pays the commission for his or her broker.

Question: Would you consider setting up a separate buyer broker real estate firm?
We can if it becomes a real factor in the marketplace. You will find us very flexible, we don't get caught up in set ways. If the market is changing, we can change on a dime and react to the market, and if that's what the marketplace is looking for we can set up a separate corporation and be buyer/ brokers very quickly.

Question: How have state-wide, mandatory disclosure forms affected your business?
I don't think it's hurt. I think it's good to let people know where you stand and what you're doing.

Question: Have disclosure forms reduced litigation?
Well, I would hope so. I guess litigation has leveled off but it has become a very litigious world and we have more law suits

in America than I would like to see. We run a good operation but there are still too many frivolous claims.

Question: Brokerage firms are usually described in terms of gross sales rather than individual incomes and company profits. Is it fair to say that of the $6.4 billion handled by Long & Foster in 1989, approximately 3 percent represented company dollars, the dollars used for rent, advertising, phones and other costs?

No it's less than 3%, it's about 1%. Close to $200 million will pass through the coffers here, but we'll keep about a third, $65 million, as company dollars.

Question: And your biggest expense is commission splits with agents?

That's right. Almost 70 percent goes out to the agents.

Question: Do you prefer to lease or own offices?

We try to be flexible. We have the capability of buying a piece of land and building our own building. We have a design, a nice federal colonial building, and we own about 20 of our sites.

The thing we like about owning is it gives us another option. We can look for a piece of ground to build on or we can look for something to lease.

Question: In conjunction with a sale handled by Long & Foster, can one of your agents earn a fee, commission, bonus or credit of any type by originating a mortgage or by providing loan information?

No.

Question: You own Prosperity Mortgage. Does that company have any special access to your agents or offices?

No. We own Prosperity Mortgage and we want our agents very much to use Prosperity Mortgage but sometimes they go out of their way not to. But little by little, as we earn the right to their business, we're getting a little higher percentage of our own business but not nearly what we would like to get. And believe me, it is strictly earned, nobody gives it to us. We're in there fighting with everyone else. We get less than 5 percent of Long & Foster's mortgage business.

Question: Does Prosperity get much business from other brokers?

A little, not a lot, it's mostly Long & Foster.

Question: Suppose in a single transaction an agent receives a fee from a buyer for loan information and also earns a commission from a seller. Can such an arrangement produce problems?

Well, if they're getting a fee, I think there can begin to be a conflict, yes. That can be trouble. It would make me very uncomfortable. That's why we take no fees from any lender or buyer.

Question: What do you look for when you hire an office manager?

Two things. Empathy and ego drive. Individuals who truly care about other people, and at the same time want to climb the ladder of success.

We will take salespeople quite often who are very driven but low on empathy because they can sell, but we try never to take a manager who is low on empathy because they'll kill you. If we have to err, we err to the side of empathy to get that person who really cares about people and loves them to death and that person—with some drive—will do wonders for you.

Question: Do you allow office managers to list and sell properties?

Usually not. In the beginning as you phase out from agent to manager, yes. As you know we build our offices to 60, 70, 80 or 90 people and you cannot list and sell if you've got that many agents to take care of.

Question: Is it possible to create another firm as large as Long & Foster?

Oh sure. When we started, there were big firms that dominated the business, but there's always somebody new coming along. If we don't work hard enough, we'll have trouble too and that's how the free market system works. It keeps us all on our toes.

SUSAN WILLETT BIRD
President
Susan W. Bird, Inc.
New York, New York

Manhattan's upscale real estate market is arguably the most unique in the country. New York brokers may not complete contracts, they have long functioned without a centralized MLS, and many sales involve cooperative units where prices are not publicly recorded or available for comparison. Rather than exclusive-right-to-sell listing arrangements, many properties are sold with open listing agreements, thus making cooperation between brokers impossible.

In 1985 Susan W. Bird, a Stanford lawyer with experience in computer sales and commercial real estate, opened a residential real estate brokerage company to service upper-bracket sellers in Manhattan. In 1988, she opened a second Manhattan firm, this one to represent buyers.

Question. Most real estate brokers operate one company. You have two brokerage firms. Why?
The first company I started represented only sellers. I was myself a seller at that time and when I looked at the market as an outsider there were lots of people running around with buyers so they appeared to be getting a lot of service. What I didn't see was anybody representing sellers so that's what I began. Not too far along people came back to us and asked, "How come you don't do a similar thing for buyers."

Question. As an attorney, do you agree that an agent should be an advocate rather than someone who is neutral?
From my perspective, I think what really happens is that in a traditionally brokered transaction, there is no real negotiation for either party. The negotiation is always intended to end up somewhere in the middle.

I often hear brokers talk about getting a meeting of the minds, but as a seller I've always felt that I was actually getting less than I could if I had my own advocate and as a buyer that I was paying more than I needed to.

I think both principals should be represented and neither of them appears to be represented now. Or they are represented in a fashion in which they can't possibly both have their interests met.

Question. Are you the broker of record for both companies?
Yes.

Question. What happens if I am a Bird buyer client and I look at properties and the only property in New York that I like is owned by a Bird seller client?
The deal is really fairly simple the way we handle it. When we talk to people and they become our clients, we explain to them that this could happen and although it's rare, at least the possibility exists. We make it clear that whoever was our client first, that is who we will represent in that transaction.

Question. As a seller's agent, your firm, any firm, is obligated to disclose whatever you know about the buyer. When a Bird buyer wants to purchase from a Bird seller, you may have gained confidential information from the purchaser during the period in which he or she was a buyer client. Do you reveal that information to a Bird seller?
The fact is that our seller's agent won't know any confidential information from the purchaser.

Question. But you ultimately are the broker?
But I wouldn't have anything to do with the transaction. I mean I am the person that runs this company.

But let's say you were the buyer. You're represented by Mary Jones, our buyer specialist. She knows nothing about the seller. She gets the same listing that every other broker in town gets about this property. If the property becomes of interest, then you will be left to your own devices if we are already representing that seller.

And our seller specialist doesn't know anything about what the buyer knows.

Question. Let's go further with this. Mary Jones does not in fact have any listing agreement with the buyer or the seller. Those agreements are with the broker, you. Whether Mary Jones is a buyer specialist or seller specialist, she doesn't have the authority to contract with a buyer or seller, only you as the broker have that authority, correct?

Yes.

Question. Isn't any broker who represents a seller obligated to tell that seller everything they can about the buyer? In other words, if the buyer discloses information, how can you keep that information from a seller?

The answer has to do with the way we deal with our clients when we take them on. What we tell a seller client, and confirm by means of a "disclosure document" given to every client, is that we are not going to reveal information that's been given to us by any buyer client.

Question. So within your contractual relationship with sellers you have built in a contingency that deals with revealing, or not revealing, information from past buyer clients?

That's right. The difficulty, in our view, is how you do this when you expand beyond being a small firm. If you're dealing with traditional brokers I think it's very tough to do.

Question. Why do you generally collect up-front fees of $1,000 to $3,000 from buyers?

To be sure that we are talking to a serious purchaser. We find that often—even though it is a very small amount of money—it's the clincher for them as to whether they're just shopping around or whether they're serious.

Question. Do you collect up-front fees from sellers?

No. We don't need to because anybody who signs our document is so tied in to us they can't move. We don't need to get their money. Unless we've made an error in pricing, we are going to sell their property.

Question. In other words, you have an exclusive-right-to-sell listing arrangement?

Right, and we only work on that basis.

Question. What's a typical transaction for you? What's a typical price?
Eight hundred thousand dollars to $1 million.

Question. Would you agree that your company is atypical compared to firms out in the suburbs or to virtually all brokerage firms?
Absolutely.

Question. What would you do if somebody wanted you to sell their $50,000 apartment in Manhattan, assuming such properties exist?
We would do a couple things. First, we would try to qualify them over the phone to see if there was something of real interest to them and to us. We're very expensive. We charge a 10-percent commission if we do a property for under $500,000.

Question. And what about above $500,000?
Above $500,000 and up to $750,000 it's 8 percent.

Question. And above that?
Six percent. Now, if somebody comes to us with a really small property, and people do—$150,000 probably is the lowest we've ever done—we will determine whether it is important for them and for us. In other words, if somebody has a really special apartment and they appear to be somebody who really gets the concept and wants to work with us, we will then dispatch somebody to do that.

The difficulty for me as the person who runs this company is that since my people don't come from the brokerage background, they are marketers, they understand that they can only deal with five or six clients at any one time. That's what our people do, so they assume that they're going to get paid on every transaction they work on. They give the same service to $150,000 seller as they do to some with a property worth $1.5 million.

Question. As an agent, isn't your obligation equal regardless of price?

It is for us. But my point is we don't take someone on if we think that we can't give them service and the smaller properties of course, are harder to do.

When we started, we were going to do an off-shoot of our normal business which we called Wings. And Wings was going to provide sellers with almost all the services of our larger company, but the difference was that we would not be there personally to show the property.

The fact is people really wanted our service and we couldn't seem to get them to say it was worth their money not to have us there, and we couldn't afford to do it.

Question. Are there brokers in New York who have unbundled services and sell on a flat fee?
Not that I know of.

Question. Are there discount brokers in New York?
There are some who are reputed to be but that is not regarded by them as something they are proud of. There is no one who has taken on the business and said "we are discounters" which I think could be useful to people.

Question. Is there peer pressure to maintain brokerage prices in the city?
I think that there is but understand that we're not really a member of this club and that our prices are higher than every one else's. I would imagine that there is such a pressure.

Question. If I went to somebody else what would I probably pay to sell an $800,000 apartment?
Five to six percent. They'd say six percent and then they'd maybe negotiate from there.

Question. You operate in what has to be one of the most peculiar markets in the country.
That's so true.

Question. Could you be successful in a smaller city where properties are less expensive?

I'd say that's not the issue. The issue might be one of size of city, because we need a certain critical mass of highly sophisticated, very busy people who see this as a value-added service.

I think the real critical thing is not so much the value of the property because we have some very savvy people who want us to work with them on a $200,000 search or a $200,000 sale. But it's more a question of the kind of person and what their expectations are of brokerage.

Question. Co-op sales are not publicly recorded because they are stock transfers rather than real estate sales. Since there is no Manhattan MLS and many of your sales involve co-op units, how do you price them?
Through building managers, our own files gathered over time, plus our own relationships.

Question. Aren't building managers often associated with competing brokers?
Almost all of them.

Question. Do they withhold information from you?
I understand from other brokers that they often withhold it from each other. Our clients, as shareholders in a co-op, generally get the information under our direction. As shareholders they have the right to that.

Question. Let's say that you're acting as a buyer broker and you buy a property listed with another company which we'll call Smith Company. Is your commission coming from the purchaser, from the seller, or the seller's broker?
Everybody who thinks about this traditionally says, well, the seller pays the commission.

The fact is the buyer has always paid the commission because it's always come out of the purchase price of that property, so it's out of his pocket that it comes.

But the obligation, the legal obligation has been on the part of the seller to pay a broker once that buyer has stepped up with the money to cover that obligation.

What I have determined from the legal readings that I

have done is that in fact—in some states but not all states—
who pays the commission is not what's crucial.

What's crucial is whether or not there has been a legal
obligation or fiduciary relationship established between the
parties.

Question. In other words, the creation of agency.
That's right. Now when we do a transaction representing a
purchaser, we give the parties a choice and the purchaser
can decide that they want to make their offer with the purchase price being one amount of money that's being paid,
and in addition to that, an amount will be paid to the buyer
broker as a commission. The seller is looking at it as a net deal
except for whatever commission he may have obligated himself to pay to the seller's broker.

*Question. So, if somebody offers $500,000 for a property owned
by Jones, the offer will say we're paying $500,000 with $450,000
going to Jones and $50,000 to our broker. Is that correct?*
Right. That's one way people can make the offer. The other
way is they say this is a $500,000 deal and you (the seller)
must obligate yourself to pay—let's say in this case $50,000—
to the broker who has represented us; and, at the close, we
want that paid out of the proceeds of sale.

*Question. The relationship between the listing broker and the
seller in virtually all cases is established before the buyer is
aware that the property is available, so isn't there a previously
existing arrangement?*
Yes.

*Question. Are you suggesting in any manner that the seller and
the seller's broker change their fee agreement?*
We don't interfere with that. What we usually find is that the
seller has already agreed—assuming there's another broker
around—that there's going to be a commission, say 6 percent,
and that half of that will go to another broker if there is one.

*Question. But it's not that it goes to "another" broker, it goes to
a subagent?*

That's right. But I'm talking about the way the seller views it. When we come on the scene with our explanation, the response that we usually get from the seller is, "Huh? Who cares? You know, as far as I'm concerned, you're just another broker."

And they are not very interested as to who I am in this whole agency discussion. And their brokers usually aren't, but I am.

Question. If listing broker Smith is dividing a 6-percent commission for a $1 million property, how are you compensated if the buyer has agreed to a higher fee, say 8 or 10 percent, for your services?

If the seller has agreed to a $60,000 commission and we are representing the purchaser, there is only $60,000 paid out at the close of this transaction.

Question. So there's no additional fee due from the buyer?
No.

Question. In effect you have a stop limit on the commission?
That's right.

Question. Let's talk about buyer brokerage commissions. Your commission is set up-front based on a sale price.
Yes.

Question. Would it be better as a buyer broker to establish a set fee up-front?

Actually, we offer several choices. Clients can pay a set amount or they can pay a percentage of the purchase price which is the traditional way things have been done on a co-brokerage basis.

Also, we have offered another approach, one where our fee would be based on how much we saved the purchaser.

Let's say that we established a price that someone was willing to pay, say $600,000. Suppose, though, that he only has to pay $550,000 because we did such a good job of negotiating for him and that we would be paid a certain percentage based on the original price and then an additional amount based on what we save him.

We had lots of people, especially Wall Street types fascinated by it. Guess how many ended up doing that? None.

Question. Have other brokers boycotted you?
Absolutely. When we first started the company. The most amazing thing as a lawyer is to see how this brokerage industry has worked because it would make antitrust lawyers lick their chops. When we set up the buyer company, we ran a full page ad and one of the major companies in the business wrote a letter saying the ad was unethical because it mentioned the words "conflict of interest" and "everyone knows that there is no conflict of interest if you represent both sides of the transaction because we've been doing it for years."

So we sent the letter to the Secretary of State's Office. And the Secretary of State's counsel sent the letter back saying "we've read your ad, and it appears to appropriately state agency law."

To quote the letter specifically, it said, "by trying to represent both parties, the real estate broker violates not only his or her fiduciary duties to the clients, the broker also demonstrates a fundamental misunderstanding of or disregard for the duties of an agent to his or her principal."

Once, when we were competing with another major firm for a listing, the seller called saying that the broker from this other firm had left a document to sign if she was to work with them. It said they would show the property to other brokers, but "not to any buyer brokerage firms."

We're the only such firm, so the seller said, "What does this mean? This doesn't sound like it would be in my interest to do that, would it?"

So then, of course, I took that letter to the head of that firm and said, "I think I have what is referred to as a smoking gun. You guys either decide that you're going to work with our buyer company or I think the Secretary of State should see this one."

And within days we then had lists of their properties and that really was the end of the difficulties.

Question. In New York as in other states, aren't agents obligated to show properties when it's in the best interest of the owner? By law?

Question. Yes.

You bet. By practice, it's another story.

Question. Around the country, some brokers are prepared to create, if the demand is there, buyer brokerage firms in addition to their seller companies, but they don't see that the demand is there. Is that a function of public education or industry education?

If you were to ask brokers in this city, they would definitely say that there's no call for it. But there is no call for it partly because brokers say, "You surely wouldn't want a buyer broker would you? Let me tell you how they work."

Question. Why use a buyer broker at all? Why not a real estate attorney or structural inspector?

I think, in many cases, that is what many people do need.

Question. In other words, that a broker could actually be eliminated from the process?

If the information were available. If you had a multiple listing service or you had some other way for people to get to that information without having to use a broker, yes.

Question. You've said that what's important for you is to have people who are good at sales as opposed to people who are good at real estate. Why is that?

I see our business as a marketing business. I really see our business as a combination of marketing and private banking in its approach. I see agents as taking on lifetime clients who establish a relationship of trust based on the sense that these people really do know what they're doing.

Now the difficulty is that I force my people to specialize truly as either buyer or seller specialists. So if they have someone with whom they've established a great relationship as a buyer and that person now wants to sell, they must refer them to a different specialist in our firm, but they then supervise that person as their client.

Question. Do they receive a referral fee?

Yes. But it's interesting. It's not unlike private banking where you go to one advisor but if you want to do real estate, jewelry, houses, whatever you want to do with that banker, he calls on a specialist who can be helpful to you, but he has the real client link and that's the way I see this business developing.

Question. In New York State, if I want to write a real estate contract, what do I do?
You get a lawyer.

Question. As a broker I can't even fill in blanks?
Not unless you are a lawyer. The fact is that although I'm a lawyer, I've also practiced both law and brokerage in the state of California where brokers do fill out forms and make contracts and the lawyers are much less involved in residential real estate transactions. And frankly, transactions there are done very professionally.

I think that the interest in the law lobby in New York in keeping brokers from doing documentation has in some way contributed to the fact that there is not a great deal of professionalism, at least in some people's eyes, among the brokers.

Question. Then it's an issue of professional territory and cash and who gets what, correct?
Yes.

Question. If I'm a broker and I have a form approved by a local real estate organization, in New York State I just can't have somebody fill in those blanks to complete an agreement?
That's right.

Question. Would you say that within real estate there is a core of very professional and adept people who would be successful at any business?
Absolutely.

Question. Traditionally one of the ways in which brokers have obtained business is through friendships, belonging to the right club, or the right church. Are such associations the best way to find a broker?

What we often tell people is that when you decide to become our client, don't do it because you like us or are our friends, you flatter us most when you say that you want to do this because you're comfortable with the process and our professionalism.

This is a business relationship and it's a serious one. That's why we document everything we do. If we were simply doing this on the basis of friendship, we'd shake your hand.

JACK R. ANDREWS
President
Help-U-Sell, Inc.
Salt Lake City, Utah

Not every real estate firm sells a single package of services. At Help-U-Sell the concept is different: charge nothing up front, assess set fees for individual services, and let clients pick from a full menu of services to create the package that's right for them.

In business since 1978, Help-U-Sell has grown to 600 franchises in 42 states as of mid-1990. A subsidiary of the Mutual Benefit Life Insurance Company of Newark, New Jersey, the firm claims that it is adding a new franchise every other day in North America.

Question. Over the years a number of brokers have sought to establish alternative fee firms and they have not succeeded. Why do you think you can be successful?
Unless you have a system, much like the business format franchise of McDonalds, just lowering fees and operating the same old way will blow apart.

Instead of driving people everywhere, giving out pumpkins and recipes, we operate more effectively. We take out all the inefficient functions that are still performed in conventional real estate.

Question. What is a franchise dollar per sale?
Well, let's take the national average, around $3,200 per sale. On that $3,200 fee a franchisee would have around $1,400 after splitting with an agent. If the sale involved a showing fee, this income is comparable to a conventional real estate office involved in a 6-percent split.

Question. Your fees are typically lower than those charged by other brokers. How do you stay in business?
A high percentage of all MLS transactions nationwide involve commission splits because two offices are involved. In other words, if the seller pays a 6-percent fee (many times it is less today), then each individual office receives 3 percent.

That 3 percent is split in each office between the broker and the agent so each earns 1.5 percent, more or less. The fees ultimately received by the office are not much different than those received by our franchisees. In addition, our franchisees should consistently do a greater volume than a conventional office.

Question. To make a property attractive to other brokers, the cooperative fee—for the sake of argument—might be 3 percent. Can't the co-op fee be larger than the commission received by your broker?
It normally is.

Question. Are you a discount broker?
No. The word discount is associated with a lower price, which also indicates a reduction in services; that's not the case with us. We've increased the services, and since we operate differently we can charge what we want.

Question. What services do you offer?
We allow the seller to choose to show their home, or we will show it. We advertise every home each week in the newspaper, guaranteed in writing. We also provide all the services offered by our fellow MLS members, all with a money-back (our fee) guaranteed at closing.

Question. The tradition in the real estate industry is that the broker holds the open house and negotiates with the purchaser. Under your system the homeowner may show the house. Who actually negotiates with the buyer, the owner or the broker?
The fact of the matter is—not only in our industry but, without exception, in every industry—when people buy things, they buy for emotional reasons and then justify their decision or verify it with the facts. Therefore, the sellers handle the most important initial communications with the buyers then the Help-U-Sell licensed agent helps with the rest.

Question. If a property is shown by an owner, when do you enter the picture?
People drive around and look at a house. If they like the

outside, they're going to go inside, aren't they? They talk with the sellers. The buyer might say, "Well, listen, I noticed the garage door's got a big hole."

The seller will say, "Don't worry, we'll fix it or adjust the price." So the basics happen right there and then. The seller picks up the phone and calls us, and they are counseled by us and know exactly what to do when things reach a certain point.

Question. How do they know when to call?
When the listing is placed, there's a seller's kit that describes everything they need to do.

Question. What if someone doesn't want to show their own home?
We can show it for them.

Question. Is it fair to say that you are really in the business of assisting FISBOs?
When you really break it down all the way, every home in this country is for sale by owner. In our industry we just happen to advertise a lot of real estate companies on the front lawn who help sellers, but every home is for sale by owner.

Question. How successful is MLS marketing?
Today almost 80 percent of all homes listed in an MLS do not sell in the initial contract period, which averages about 120 days. Even though 70 to 80 percent of all properties are sold by MLS, it is because there has not been a viable option before.

Question. The real estate industry heavily promotes the MLS concept. Where do you find evidence of such poor results?
Each of our approximately 600 offices in 42 states are members of the MLS and provide us with monthly reports.

Question. What percentage of your clients take the MLS option?
About 10 percent.

Question. Do other brokers cooperate with you?
It's not unusual to have 20 percent of our listings sold by other brokers. They understand if a buyer wants a Help-U-Sell house they had better help the buyer or he/she will go directly to the owner.

Question. Let's look at it differently. Do your franchisees sell properties listed by other brokers?
Approximately 20 to 30 percent of our business results from working with buyers who buy someone else's listings.

Question. As this is written in mid-1990, would you acknowledge that a national slowdown in real estate sales would naturally lead to longer selling times, both for MLS listings and for properties in general?
It's obviously more of a buyer's market nationwide right now.

Question. Does that make an argument that your firm should also represent purchasers as buyer brokers?
That's a good argument, and, in fact, we've had a buyer's agreement for about 10 years. It's a perfect fit for our company.

Question. What percentage of all purchasers do you think are represented by realty brokers?
Probably less than 5 percent of all sales that take place.

Question. Should agents receive fees for loan information and placements?
If you were licensed as a mortgage broker and if the state allowed you to do that, you certainly could, especially with disclosure. If the rate was fair and the buyer felt comfortable, it would help to put the transaction together, but I don't see that function happening in the industry with a typical real estate agent. I think it has to be a specialist who handles that separately from the real estate agent. It could be in the same facility, however.

Question. Suppose you take a loan application. Would you have to reveal its contents to a seller since you represent owners in the usual case?
Your obligation as an agent would be to that seller all the way. Whether that obligation extends to disclosing the finances of a buyer prior to or during an offer are questionable. There is no question that a buyer's and a seller's interest can be totally opposite as to price.

Question. Can your brokers sell insurance or other products?
Some of our brokers sell other products. Property and casualty insurance and homeowners warranties are sold.

Question. Where do you find brokers and agents?
Perhaps 70 percent come from traditional real estate, and another 30 percent come from outside real estate or are newly licensed.

Question. How much compensation do your agents receive?
I would feel comfortable representing to you that it is significantly more than the national average for active licensees with MLS membership.

Question. How much are franchisees required to contribute for advertising?
Seven percent. They get a statement every month showing how much they paid in and how much they have available.
If it's a buyer's market, they're going to use 10 or 12 different messages. If it's a seller's market, they will use other messages. These are pieces of a system which has proven to work in good and bad markets.

Question. What does a franchise cost?
The average cost is $20,000 with a 50-percent downpayment and the balance financed over five years.

Question. Is your franchise fee based on population?
Yes, $345 per 1,000 people.

Question. Do many of your franchisees fail?
A very small percentage close due to personal problems,

partnership difficulties, or because they don't follow the system.

Question. Why do you call your agents "counselors?"
We call our licensed agents "counselors" because the public resents salespeople and sales pressure, so the counseling role is more that of a doctor or any professional where you gather information and solve problems.

Question. Since you charge less than other brokers, how do you generate profits?
More volume. Our economics are different since we generate all the buyers and sellers without anybody going out and literally knocking on doors, holding open houses, or any of that.

Buyers and sellers call our office so floor time is valuable. Our counselors will come in with the flu rather than miss floor time because that's where buyer leads and seller leads come from. What you'll find is that we spend a little more on the advertising to make this happen, but on the other side of it, we don't have to worry about an agent taking business out the door by asking for 80, 90 or 100 percent commissions because they can all leave and the buyers and sellers will still call our office.

That's why we like newly-licensed people; we want people coming in who will just work the system because the system brings them the buyers and sellers.

Question. Can franchisees make additional money showing the house?
Yes, another $500 to $1000 depending on what market they're in. Upwards of 30 percent of our sales involve us showing the property.

Question. How many sales will you handle this year?
It would be very tough to give you an exact figure, but we might have 90,000 transaction sides this year.

Question. Does your approach work in soft markets?
You're competing with all the inventory out there but by

kicking out some of that commission, that extra cost, we can help sellers achieve the same net and a faster sale.

As far as buyers, they come into the market with only so much for a downpayment and they're going to look at every single home because there's no urgency in a soft market. They're looking for the greatest selection, and when they see "by owner" it kind of registers as a better value to them.

So, as buyers, the less you pay, the less the outstanding mortgage. A lower mortgage means lower monthly payments, and it is easier to qualify for the home you want. That's where our system really excels and why we have typically gained market share in soft times.

Question. Is the independent broker being squeezed and, if so, by who?

Well, it depends who comes into their market, who's their competition, because most independent brokers are built around a person and their name and relationships. When somebody comes into that market who will match their service but give greater value, the independents will have to make a change. You now see that not only independents but conventional franchise owners are being squeezed and have to change. This is why we are now expanding while conventional brokerages (independents and franchises) are contracting.

PART IV
Words from the Past

Much of this book considers how the real estate industry will evolve, an analysis derived from selected trends and tendencies and one that raises a basic question: Just how reliable are such projections? As astrologers, fortune tellers and economists have proven with equal skill, looking into the future is hardly a science and no claim can be made that infallible guidance will be found on these pages, or elsewhere.

In fairness, though, it should also be said that past projections have often been reasonably prescient. Ten years ago the real estate industry was in ferment. Recent court cases had pushed brokerage into the realm of interstate commerce and thus federal oversight. Corporate goliaths were buying out large regional brokers to assemble nationally-known chains and franchises were one of the hottest movements in real estate.

What did it all mean? With as much luck as foresight, the following article appeared in *The Washington Post* on April 4, 1981. Originally entitled, "Real Estate Brokers: Avoiding the Big Guy," I wrote it in response to an article predicting the small broker's demise, a future that seemed as unlikely then as it does today.

Real Estate Brokerage: Predictions from 1981

One of the major trends of the past decade has been the gradual movement toward larger economic units in many industries. Companies merge, conglomerates grow and more and more frequently small business lacks the economies of scale necessary to compete.

The argument has been made ("The Mom and Pop Real Estate Business Nears Extinction," *The Washington Post* March 21, 1981) that independent real estate practitioners will be largely out of business by 1990, replaced by a coterie of huge, centralized companies and a web of national franchises. Real estate brokers of today, it is suggested, are much like the small grocery stores of the past which have now been replaced by major supermarket chains.

Unlike food distribution or the manufacture of widgets or whatever, real estate brokerage is a personal service business, similar to the practice of law or accounting where individual skills, delivered locally, are a major factor in the marketplace.

In much the same manner that the Big Eight accounting firms handle much of the business associated with Fortune 500 companies, there is a need for larger firms in real estate. Major companies have the resources and skills to handle specialized services, such as subdivision sales and condominium development, which are not practical or attractive business opportunities for individual practitioners or smaller firms.

Substantial brokerage organizations already exist in most major cities, and often have 30 offices and more than 500 agents. Such firms encompass virtually all the qualities one would expect to find in a national realty corporation with localized operations. Yet, even with large-scale competitors here today, independent practitioners and small firms are still marketing their services successfully. Looking toward the future, there are institutional issues which suggest a competitive environment not far different from that which now exists in many urban areas.

First, there is great mobility among successful realty agents. Top individuals consistently move to new firms or establish their own brokerage operations. Will conglomerates hold top agents. If so, at what cost?

Second, as a result of the McLain decision in the Supreme Court last year, a case which established that brokerage activities are within the "stream" of interstate commerce, will there be fair and open pricing competition among real estate brokers? Will smaller firms, with less overhead, be more competitive as more and more sellers negotiate fees?

Third, will realty services become increasingly unbundled? Larger firms may enjoy significant profits by offering services to both sellers and buyers. For example, a firm may broker a seller's property and later earn a fee by locating a mortgage for a purchaser. Aren't such services in conflict? The Maryland attorney general has given an opinion that a conflict does exist in such situations, one which is not permitted under state law.

Fourth, as firms become larger will the labor market change? Will unions seek to organize agents? Will new tax rulings challenge the independent status now given to agents, a status that frees brokers from the responsibility of paying unemployment or Social Security taxes?

One possible response to large-scale competitors can be found in the growing franchise movement. A survey of 1,000 members by the National Association of Realtors (NAR) shows that approximately 19 percent of its brokers are affiliated with such groups.

Franchises are designed to give member firms enhanced name recognition and thus a competitive edge. The NAR survey indicates that many, though far from all, franchise members are satisfied with their organizations. As with brokerage generally, franchises have been affected by the overall economic problems which have been influencing realty sales nationwide.

The number of franchisers has begun to spawn, amoeba-like, until today it is estimated that there are more than 75 such organizations throughout the country. Not only are there more franchisers but many are becoming individually larger as well.

As franchise organizations grow it can be argued that they lose the element of exclusivity that made them attractive in the first place. Will brokers pay a premium to belong to organizations that are increasingly indistinct? Will the franchise movement itself be dampened as vast numbers of franchisers meld together in the public mind?

The assumption is often made that colossal economic enterprises somehow possess infinite financial wisdom as well as superior competitive strengths. This is not always the case as shareholders of W.T. Grant, Penn Central, Chrysler and other corporate giants can attest.

As long as real estate brokerage remains a localized, personal service business it seems likely that independent practitioners and smaller firms will continue to compete. Somehow, one suspects that in 1990 the phone directory will still contain pages of brokers rather than the names of just a few elephantine institutions.

Index